URGENCY

MAKING A DIFFERENCE
IN THE WORLD

KEITH JOSEPH

dustjacket

dustjacket
www.dustjacket.com

CONTENTS

Introduction.. v

Chapter One: Who's with Us?.................................... 1

Chapter Two: A Significant Moment........................... 9

Chapter Three: The Voices of Our Day...................... 17

Chapter Four: Losing Sight of the Why...................... 23

Chapter Five: Tribulation Trail 31

Chapter Six: A Church in a Difficult Place 39

Chapter Seven: Tolerance 47

Chapter Eight: The Church that Fell Asleep 53

Chapter Nine: The Unstoppable Church.................... 61

Chapter Ten: Voices at the Door............................... 67

Chapter Eleven: Changing Your Outlook................... 75

Week Twelve: A Shifting Culture.............................. 83

Chapter Thirteen: Easter, The Answer for All Your Fears 91

Chapter Fourteen: Fire on the Earth.......................... 99

Chapter Fifteen: Urgent Spiritual Updates................ 105

Chapter Sixteen: Who Will be Christ in Our Most Crucial Hour? 111

Chapter Seventeen: Making Sense Out of Life, Pt. 1 119

Chapter Eighteen: Making Sense Out of Life, Pt. 2........ 127

Chapter Nineteen: Making Sense Out of Life, Pt. 3 135

Chapter Twenty: The Last Round, Getting What We Deserve 141

Chapter Twenty-One: Whose Side are You On? 149

Chapter Twenty-Two: The Day We Live For................................ 157

Chapter Twenty-Three: A Different Leader and a Different World 165

Chapter Twenty-Four: God's Courtroom, The Final Judgement... 173

Chapter Twenty-Five: Living Between Two Worlds..................... 181

Chapter Twenty-Six: I'm Going Home.. 189

Chapter Twenty-Seven: What Are My Options? 197

Conclusion.. 205

Works Cited 211

As I sat down in my seat, no one knew the stress in my heart and mind. Part of my stress was selfish in nature because I had just been told that our bags for our mission trip would not be transferred to our next plane. We were told we would have to receive our bags at the next airport and recheck them before our next flight. I realized as I buckled my seat belt, this was an impossible task. But deeper still was the question: Was I really making a difference in the world?

I cried out to God with a simple question, am I making a difference? I was assuming, if I was making a difference, things would be easy. But that truly was not the case, and it never is the case.

In that moment, my mind was diverted from my problem because our plane began to take off. It was a very rainy and cloudy morning. I looked out my window wondering what God was up-to. I wondered even more if what I was doing was worth it. As our plane entered the clouds, I thought, this is my life right now. I am in the clouds and I do not know where all of this is headed, and I have zero clue how it will turn out.

Suddenly it happened, our plane broke through the clouds. The sun began to shine on my face. Immediately I was warmed not only in my body but in my spirit. I felt the peace of Heaven. I knew the Lord had everything under control. I knew I was making a difference because I was telling others about the light of Jesus Christ.

Certainly, our day is a day filled with dark clouds. These are days where most people are living their lives in the darkness without understanding where they are headed. For most there is zero urgency about their future. However, for those of us who call ourselves Christ-followers, this has become a day of urgency. Truly this is a day when many in the church want to make a difference in the world.

It is this way with many young Christ followers. My youngest son, John, is now planning for his life. The burning question on his heart is not what should I do, but how can I make a difference right now? Here are John's own words, they speak volumes about many in their teenage years, "I don't want to waste time preparing to make a difference, I want to make a difference." This is the cry of someone who is feeling a true urgency.

Webster defines the word urgency as "a force or impulse that impels or constrains." As a pastor I feel the urgency of Heaven leading me to an urgency in my life as a Christ-follower. I sense the Lord giving the church a door of opportunity for the everlasting gospel, Rev. 3:3. I feel like Paul did as he wrote to the church at Corinth, "For a great and effective door has opened to me, and there are many adversaries," I Cor. 16:9.

The question that comes to my mind is this: will the church as a whole respond to the urgency of our day? Will the church rise up above the clouds of darkness to see what God's plans are for our day? Will the church embrace the vision of making a difference in the world now? Will the church come alongside this generation and storm the gates of Hell making a difference now?

Maybe you ask, how is it possible to make a difference now? We find the answer in the one true place where God's answers are always found. The place is the Bible. On every page we find God's plan for today and for the future. The book you hold in your hand focuses on one book of the Bible, the book of Revelation. The book of Revelation reveals God's plan for the church now and His plan for the future. If there is a book of the Bible that fuels our urgency it is the book of Revelation. The book of Revelation teaches us how to make a difference in the world now.

For many people, the book of Revelation seems like a lost cause because its content seems beyond understanding. The late Adrian Rogers took issue with the historian H.G. Wells, who wrote a book entitled *The Fate of Man*, in which he said, "Who, except cranks and lunatics, reads the Book of Revelation." Here was Dr. Rogers' response:

> "I must disagree. God has given us divine insight
> into the future and a message in the Book of Revelation
> that He is in control. God is not wringing His hands
> in heaven and wondering what He is going to do. The
> Holy Trinity never meets in emergency session. God is
> in control." (Adrian Rogers, *Unveiling the End Times*
> *in our Times*, [Nashville Tn, Broadman, and Holman],
> 2004 Pg. 5, "*Unveiling the End Times in our Time.*"

Many people have turned the book of Revelation into something that God did not intend. I must warn you of those who have written books seeking to find the secret codes of Revelation. Such people make wild predictions, and they make unbelievable comparisons. You and I will stay away from such unproductive efforts. We will read and study this book together with the purpose of fueling our urgency as well as fueling our plan of action in these dark days we live in. We will discover over and over again how we can make a difference in the world now.

If you have a burning desire to make a difference in the world, this book is for you. If you feel the urging of God to make a difference now, this book is for you. If you are tired of the merry-go-round of life, this book is for you.

I have written this book because I also feel the urgency of God to make a difference in the world. I must confess that I could not have accomplished this without the Holy Spirit and God's Word. But I could also not have accomplished this without two other people. I give thanks for my Executive Pastor, Cary Snelling, who spent countless hours debating, challenging, and stretching me to be firmly convinced of what I was writing. He has had profound impact on this book. I also want to thank my Administrative Assistant, Kellie Medlin, whose daily labor to keep my office free from interference as well as her hours of proofing this book are seen on every page. Finally I want to thank Betty Carter (a second-mother to me) who labored many hours in editing the final product. Thanks to each of you for fueling my urgency for the Gospel.

I want to challenge you to dive deep in this study with me! In each chapter we will be reminded of God's great urgent call on our lives. One verse from this great book says it all for me. Revelation 14:6

⁶Then I saw another angel flying directly overhead, with an eternal gospel to proclaim to those who dwell on earth, to every nation and tribe and language and people.

With urgency God has called His church to carry the eternal Gospel to the ends of the earth in this our day.

Our Lord's blessing is promised as we make this journey together. I challenge you to ascend with me above the clouds of darkness and allow the light of God's glorious Word to fill your hearts and minds with His truth that will direct our paths in these days. Let me plead with you to understand what others have understood: This book is for the purpose to fuel your urgency to reach souls with the gospel.

One last note: this book will be different than any other I have written. You will see a companion reading plan at the end of the book that I encourage you to follow. But in our studies, I have given you questions to answer within the text of each chapter we cover. These questions will challenge you both theologically and practically.

As always, my goal is that you would use this book as a resource in your small group time or in your personal devotions. In no way do I want this to replace you study of God's Word. This book is a tool to enhance your study.

The church I pastor, FBC Jackson, is taking this journey with us. If we can help you in any way, please contact us a www. Jacksonfbc.com.

May God bless you with an urgency from Him during your time of study.

Pastor Keith,

Phil. 1:27, "Only let your manner of life
be worthy of the gospel of Christ...."
August 2019

CHAPTER ONE

Who's with Us?

REVELATION 1:1-3

*"Arm yourselves, and be ye men of valor,
and be in readiness for conflict."*

The leaders gathered in a room waiting for the commander to arrive. The mood in the room was dark and the silence was deafening. The future of the free world seemed to be hanging in the balance. Many in the room wanted to attempt to make peace with the enemy. But wiser leaders knew there was no peace to be had with the enemy. As the leaders waited, the reports began to come in about smaller and weaker nations falling one after another. The silence was now almost more than the leaders could handle. Most believed their nation would be next.

It was in this dark moment when the commander walked into the room. With the utmost of confidence, Winston Churchill began to speak. By the time he had finished speaking, the mood in the room had changed. Many in the room now embraced the view, we will win this war. In his first nationwide broadcast as prime minister, on May 19, 1940, Churchill is quoted as having said:

"Arm yourselves, and be ye men of valor, and be in readiness for conflict; for it is better for us to perish in battle than to look upon the outrage of our nation and our altar. As the will of God is in Heaven, even so let it be." (Jonathan Sandys & Wallace Henley, *God and Churchill* [Tyndale Momentum Publishing, 2015], 86)

To those who lived in that era of history, the war was real, and for many, Winston Churchill was their only source of hope.

As I write this chapter, there is another war being raged in the world. The enemy seems to be claiming more and more territory. As I write this chapter, the largest sex-trafficking network in the world exists just 60 miles from me in Atlanta, with much of the church world doing nothing. Six states have ratified abortion on demand, and most states are facing legislation to legalize same-sex marriage.

For those who hold true to God's standards outlined in His Word, it seems as if the standards are toppling as one denomination at a time rolls over to a liberal view. The voice of the church that should be louder than ever, seems to be quieter than ever. The false doctrines of our day are shouting we are to love others, when in truth they are shouting tolerance at the cost of truth. Jesus did not go to the cross so that we would preach a message of tolerance. Jesus went to the cross so that we could be transformed to live in truth (Romans 12:1-2).

I have a question: Who will lead us to victory in these dark days? Who will stand up and be accounted as God's voice in these days? Who will stand up in board meeting rooms and in business meetings and cry out thus says the Lord? It is time for the church to get back to carrying out the mandate of gospel saturation instead of the mess of gospel slaughter.

Now before I get ahead of myself, I want to take you back in time to another room where leaders were waiting. The mood in that room was dark as well. Those who gathered there had their hopes and plans crushed just three days earlier as their leader had been arrested, tried, convicted, and executed.

There were rumors that their leader had been seen alive, but how could he be? He truly had been executed. One of the leaders tried to rally the team. He said that the place where they laid him was empty. One of the team members said they saw him alive. What kind of leader could this be, who would die and be raised from the dead?

His name? Jesus. For three plus years, Jesus had been the leader of the group (John 17:7-8). But in this Upper Room, the team was devastated. However, within a few moments, the mood in the room was about to change, because their leader was about to come into the room (John 20).

I cannot imagine the joy that came to that leadership room as the team heard from their leader. The Bible teaches us that for the next forty days Jesus prepared His leaders for a transition in leadership. Jesus was going to return to His command center in heaven. The team would take charge of the operations on the ground. The team did not have to worry. Jesus was sending a Helper (Acts 1:8) to direct them on the ground.

On day forty Jesus left (Acts 1:11), and on day fifty the Helper came (Acts 2). Now it was the time for the plan to be carried out. So was the story of the beginning of the church. For two thousand plus years the church has flourished in good times and in bad times, with its influence continuing despite all odds.

It seems as we look back over church history that there were many moments when someone was called to be the voice of urgency for the church. There were those who, at the risk of their own lives, were willing to make a difference in the world. That voice was placed upon a newly converted monk in the sixteenth century by the name of Martin Luther.

Once Luther stood before an assembly (The Diet at Worms) to give an account for his urgent break from traditional Catholic views. Here is what he said:

> "My conscience is captive to the Word of God. I will not recant anything, for to go against conscience is neither honest nor safe. Here I stand, I cannot do otherwise. God help me. Amen." (Bruce Shelly, *Church History in Plain Language* [Nashville: Thomas Nelson Publishing, 2013], 254)

Now five-hundred years later, the church faces one of its toughest tests as the world is spinning out of control while the church seems to be more in retreat and redefining mode, when she should be in revival and reaching out mode.

All around us there are failing attempts at getting better. The halls of Congress have become a warzone of hate and division. The family unit is facing a re-orientation of order and purpose. Sexuality is bombarded with alternative lifestyles. The church is being forced to decide whether to embrace the new way of looking at the Bible or to stand strong on the traditional view of the Word of God.

This very morning, I have just come from a leadership meeting where the leaders in the room were all pastors. Many of them were discouraged about the above issues along with many more. Some even said, "Our congregation does not seem to even notice what is happening to our world." Another person told of a pastor from another state who said, "If I stand for what I believe, I will possibly lose my job."

Brothers and sisters, in my heart there is a strong urgency stirring. I believe the church does not have to retreat, give in, hide out, or lash out in hate. I believe our best days are ahead of us. I feel the urgent call of God to carry the everlasting gospel (Rev. 14:6) to a world at war. I believe God is raising up a new generation of believers who are genuinely committed to making a difference in the world now.

It seems to me there are more opportunities today than there have ever been to engage this world. But we must be honest, this urgent call will be costly to us personally. I believe this was the same scenario facing the church as they neared the end of the first century.

I want you to travel with me back in time to a day when the church was going through transition. The church was being led by second and third generation believers. The leaders who had gathered in the upper room were all gone except the Apostle John.

John had paid a great price for his stand for the Lord. He was, at the time of his writing the book of Revelation, by conservative estimates, around 90 years of age. He had been exiled (1:9) to a barren, volcanic island in the Aegean Sea, about forty miles offshore from Miletus. MacArthur writes about this day:

> "Exile to such islands was a common form of punishment in the first century. John was probably sent there as a criminal because he was a Christian, considered in that day as an illegal religious sect. He would have been under harsh labor with the most brutal of conditions." John MacArthur, *MacArthur New Testament Commentary, Revelation, Vol 1* [Chicago: Moody Publishers, 1999], 41)

It is here where John received an urgent message from the Lord. We know this message to be the book of Revelation. The word "revelation" speaks of an unveiling of things not known before. Webster's defines it as "a surprising and previously unknown fact."

John was given this revelation to communicate with the church. John's purpose was clear. He was to communicate the following:

- To reveal to the church "God in His glorious justice and mercy revealed through judgment." (James M. Hamilton, *Preaching the Word in Revelation* [Wheaton, IL: Crossway Publishing, 2012], 18)

- To reveal what will happen in the days leading up to Jesus' Second-Coming.

- To mobilize the church to actively engage in sharing the everlasting gospel with the world.

As John begins to write, he is recruiting churches to join in the mobilization of actively engaging in sharing the everlasting gospel with the world.

The first three verses are John's prologue which is simply his way of orienting the readers with the content of the coming book. In the chapters to come, you and I will journey with John as he outlines every part of the message he received from Jesus Christ. John wants his readers to know that he left out nothing, and he added nothing to the message he received. This is exactly how he received it.

John ends the prologue with a simple promise and an urgent plea. The simple promise is the blessing of God to those who read the message and carry out the battle plan in the message. The urgent plea is to carry out the battle plan because "the time is near" (1:3).

I want to ask you; will you take the time to read the entire message with a heart to learn? And will you join the team called the church who is being called to an urgent response in these last days? If you are joining the team, keep on reading because urgency is about to be released into your heart and mind. Yes, you will face hard moments, but the hard times will turn out to be a blessing in the glorious work of Christ in you and through you. To those who are still on the fence I ask, will you take the journey with me? At least keep on reading and see what God says.

STUDY QUESTIONS:

1. What is the purpose of Revelation in God's plan?
2. Is God still giving new revelation?
3. Describe how you feel and how you usually respond when revelation is given to you?
4. Why is our world in desperate need of God's revelation?
5. In what ways can revelation make you a more ntentional believer?
6. Write down five things you know about the book of Revelation?
7. What did John mean by, "the time is near"?
8. What is the number one problem in our world today?

CHAPTER TWO

A Significant Moment

REVELATION 1:4-8

"Why are you not writing anything down?"
Lindswell whispered.
"There is nothing being said, worth writing down,"
Bridgeman whispered back.

I n May 1940, the remnants of the French and British armies retreated to Dunkirk. 338,000 were trapped on the beach. Hitler's armies were pressing in for the final kill. Walter Lord writes, "Unable to retreat any farther, the Allied soldiers set up defense positions and prayed for deliverance." (Walter Lord, *The Miracle of Dunkirk* [New York, N.Y.: Open Road Media, 1982], 80). It was a very significant moment in the lives of these soldiers.

As the men waited and prayed, there was a leadership meeting taking place. The general in charge began to make plans for a counterattack, but all knew it was a waste of time to even talk about such attempts. It was so ridiculous that the solider who was taking notes did not write anything down. When asked why he was not writing anything down, he responded: "There is nothing being said, worth writing down."

As the church approached the turn of the first century, their situation seemed to be almost as desperate as the situation in Dunkirk. Yes, there were strong churches like the churches in Philadelphia and Smyrna, but others were like the church in Sardis (3:1) that seemed to be alive but was dead. There were also the many churches that struggled with false teachers. For many, there was not much being said that was worth writing down.

In the twenty-first century we see the same dynamic in the local church. There are churches who are truly thriving in doing the work of the Lord. But there are also dying churches, and there are many pretending churches who have a reputation of being alive, but they are dead. You ask, how do you know? Just look around where their churches are located. Has crime gone down? Are the homeless being cared for? Are the crack-houses closing? Do we see the light of the gospel shining? It almost seems that the church has lost its power in the world. The watching world does not seem to be taking notice about what we have to say.

Steve Gaines commented in a recent sermon: "The hope of America does not lie in the White House, but in the church house." He went on the say, "Without the church, America has no hope." (Gaines, Steve. "Godly People Love God," January 8, 2019)

Something must take place within the churches in America if we are going to turn things around. Without a message from heaven, the world will continue to ignore, and in many cases, persecute the church.

The message from heaven that will bring urgency is the book of Revelation. Today we come to the greeting section of the book. Dr. Hamilton reminds us of the urgent purpose:

"Jesus intends for this urgent message to produce a radical change in perspective. He intends the persecuted members of these lowly and insignificant churches to feel the reality that they are blessed. In spite of the fact that they are at odds with the reigning culture of the Roman Empire, in spite of the hostility of the Emperor and Satan himself. The church was blessed." (Hamilton, 34)

The blessing was in what they were about to read. This was a significant moment in their lives, and God intends it to be a significant moment in our lives. Just as the soldiers were praying in Dunkirk for a miracle, you and I need this same miracle from heaven.

In this significant moment in time, John reminds us of three miracle truths:

GOD HAS NOT CHANGED, VS: 4-5

The world is always changing, but God has not changed. The seven churches who received this letter needed to be reminded of this truth. Be assured these were literal churches in that day, and they also symbolically represent the church as a whole in every age. The number seven speaks of completion. Every generation needs to be reminded of this truth: God has not changed.

This God who has not changed offers every true church both grace and peace. Grace is how we get into the family of God (Eph. 2:8) and peace describes our position with God (Rom. 5:1) once we are in the family. The church desperately needs grace and peace.

In John's day, the churches needed grace and peace. For example, the church in Smyrna would soon face extreme tribulation (2:10-11).

The church would so need the peace of the God (Phil. 4:6-7). Steve Lawson wrote:

> "God Himself is peace, Eph. 2:14. Peace exclusively belongs to Him alone. This is a peace of the soul that is an inner calm that settles the turbulence of troubled hearts. It is unnatural, flooding our hearts, drowning out worry. When a believer prays, God may not change their circumstances, but he does change their heart." (Steve Lawson, *Philippians For You* [North America, The Good Book Company, 2017], 197)

The church needed grace and peace as they came to a day of urgency in the world.

As we read about God, we are reminded of the work of the Trinity in bringing grace and peace.

Wayne Grudem defines the Trinity as follows: "God eternally exists as three persons, Father, Son, and Holy Spirit, and each person is fully God, and there is one God." (Wayne Grudem, *Systematic Theology* (536)

We read of God the Father, "Who is, who was, and who is to come." God the Father has always existed. He exists now, firmly in control of the universe. He will exist in the days to come, because He is God. The church never has to fear being overthrown by the enemy.

Ruling with the Father is the Holy Spirit, represented here symbolically by the seven spirits. The Holy Spirit regenerates the believer (Titus 3:5); resides in the believer (I Cor. 12:3); and represents Jesus on the earth (John 16:3-11). It is the Holy Spirit who empowers us to live the Christian Life.

Along with the Father and the Holy Spirit is Jesus, who is identified by three actions in his earthly ministry: He is the faithful witness, the first-born from the dead, and the ruler of the kingdoms. In a day of lies, scandals, and broken leadership, Jesus stands alone as totally reliable, the pioneer of the resurrection of the dead, and the coming sovereign ruler of the universe.

These three make up the Trinity. God is the one hope of this world. In a day of superstar preachers and religious trickery, we have true hope only in God. It is for this God that we want to make a difference in this world.

GOD IS ALWAYS AT WORK.

As John continues to write, he focuses in on Jesus, who is always at work. John reminds the church of the eternal and never ceasing love of Jesus. Let this truth soak in today as you face those moments when the Devil lies by saying you are all alone. Jesus is for you (Romans 8:31), and Jesus loves you with an everlasting love (Jeremiah 31:3). He loves this generation of believers as much as He loved the first century church (Psalm 105:17).

It was said that when Winston Churchill understood the dire emergency of the soldiers in Dunkirk he said, "If we could get a few hundred out, it would be a miracle." He did not understand the power of love in a nation that would come together to rescue all those soldiers. I believe we often fail to understand how the God-head came together in love for us.

We see this love in Jesus, purchasing our freedom by His own blood (I John 1:7). Jesus left His secure place in heaven and came into the war zone of this world for us. His work was completed on Easter weekend over two-thousand years ago. The cross and the empty tomb tell the story of God's work for us. But He has not stopped working (Heb. 1:2-4).

Jesus is building us a new home in the Kingdom of Heaven (John 14:6). He has given the church ministry to accomplish in this world. Brothers and sisters, if God is at work, we are called to be at work as well. It is our time to join him in the work. Souls are on the beaches of life about to be destroyed by the enemy. It is time for urgency in our day. You and I can make a difference in the world as part of His army.

GOD IS COMING AGAIN.

Brothers and sisters the announcement in verses 6 and 7 must have come as welcome news to a people who were living and dying while wondering when Jesus would come again. You and I still wonder this today. But we are encouraged to know that He is a God of truth. He will keep His Word, and He is coming again. Every eye will see Jesus. This will be a day of great triumph for the church. But it will be a great tragedy for those who rejected Him.

I cannot imagine what it will look like when Jesus returns. The scene in Revelation 19 speaks of both triumph and tragedy when He returns. I look to that day, and it drives me to urgency because this could be my last day.

These three truths should revive each of us, and I pray they revive the church in America. May this moment be significant to each who read this chapter. Take time this week to focus on what this means to you, to the church, and to the world.

STUDY QUESTIONS:

1. What does the average American think about God?

2. Do you ever wonder if God sometimes forgets you in difficult moments? Explain your answer.

3. How would this text help you in counseling someone who believes God does not care?

4. Name some social issues that need God's attention.

5. Why do we sometimes fear sharing our faith in hostile environments?

6. Describe what John meant by "a kingdom of priests."

7. Share with the group how God gives peace in your life.

8. When will Jesus return? Explain and defend your answer.

CHAPTER THREE

The Voices of Our Day

REVELATION 1:9-20

"I'm learning from the most powerful voice of my generation,"
—Chris Mann, 2012 finalist for "The Voice."

Chris Man shared the above quote on his twitter feed about his voice coach, Christina Aguilera. When I read this, I took a moment and Googled some of Christina's hit songs. Here are a few lyrics from her 2002 hit song "Dirty": "dirty, filthy, nasty, you nasty, too dirty to clean my act up, if you ain't dirty, you ain't here to party, ladies, move, gentlemen move, somebody ring the alarm, fire on the roof."

Am I the only one shaking my head at this moment? Is this the type of voice that has the ear of our nation? The twenty-first century has become a century driven by the opinions of men. If a person has access to Wi-Fi, he or she has the capability of having a voice throughout our nation.

As a follower of Jesus Christ, I find it extremely troubling to listen to the voices of our day. The voices of our day often come from people whose views are formed in a world system filled with unrighteous theories of life.

Far too often the views of our day are left unchecked by truth. We often read of people whose careers have been destroyed by unfounded voices. Such voices have damaged others and have damned many to eternity apart from God.

When the church is confronted with giving an answer to such voices, often we have either become cynical or silent in our response. I truly believe the church needs a reformation of truth. Martin Luther believed this in his day. He is quoted as saying, "Human reason is like a drunken man on horseback; set him up on one side, and he tumbles over on the other."

The prophet Jeremiah wrote of his day:

> "They bend their tongue like a bow; falsehood and not truth has grown strong in the land; for they proceed from evil to evil, and they do not know me, declares the LORD.
>
> Everyone deceives his neighbor, and no one speaks the truth; they have taught their tongue to speak lies; they weary themselves committing iniquity." (Jeremiah 9:3,5.)

Does not this sound familiar in our day? I write this chapter with the greatest of urgency, believing in the need for a reformation of our voices in the church. In his day, the Apostle John had heard the voice of God (I John 1:1-3). John walked with Jesus, saw His miracles, and heard Him teach daily for over three years. Now John is ninety years old. He has been speaking about the voice of God, and he has been giving witness to the life of Jesus.

For sixty years, his was a voice for God. Now that voice had cost him greatly. If you had seen John in that day you would have noticed the severe burns to his body from being burned in oil. But through it all, John would not let his voice be silent, because too much was at stake.

In 2018, Pastor Ramin Parsa was arrested in the Mall of America for simply sharing his faith with two people who held Muslim viewpoints. This pastor was arrested simply for responding to the question, "Why did you leave the Muslim faith and embrace Christianity?" Question: Is speaking for Jesus really that important?

The Apostle John believed so. It has been sixty years since the day he saw Jesus taken up into heaven. Revelation 1:9 zooms in on a particular Sunday as John was worshiping the Lord. We do not know what he was doing, but we do know that most likely it was forced labor, but in the Spirit of the Lord. As he worked and worshiped, suddenly a voice as clear as a trumpet being blown in the early morning came into John's ears. The voice gives John a clear command, "write…"

I believe John recognized the voice. It had been sixty years since he had last heard this audible voice. But it was still fresh in his mind. John turns to see if it is true. Is this voice, the voice of the One he thinks it is? John turns to see, and to His joy, it is the Son of Man in His glorified state.

The description John gives to us is one I try to visualize in my mind over and over. Is this imagery or is this exactly how Jesus looks? I believe it must be a mixture of both. Here we are able to see Jesus as our true priest and king. I see Him standing there robed with righteous garments. There He stands in spotless purity signified by His hair being white as wool. He stands there with eyes as of fire. He is the all-knowing God whose feet remind us of His untarnished integrity. No one ever compares to Jesus.

Next, John tries to describe His voice. Do you hear the roar of Niagara Falls? The voice of Jesus speaks with authority and power. The church does not need to fear the voice of men. The voice of God is stronger still.

Do you see Him standing there as our majestic Lord and Savior? There is no one like Him. It is His voice the world desperately needs to hear.

In this moment John bows before Him as one who falls at someone's feet as if dead. I want to pause and share with you the first of two things one must have if he or she is going to bow and obey the voice of God:

ONE MUST HAVE AN AWE FOR GOD.

John bows as one who loves and respects Jesus. In John's life, there was no one who occupied the place Jesus occupied. He knew that eternal life resided in Jesus (I John 1:2). He knew Jesus had given eternal life to him. John was in AWE of God.

John ended His gospel with the following commentary: "Now there are also many other things that Jesus did. Were every one of them to be written, I suppose that the world itself could not contain the books that would be written." (John 21:25)

This is a man who has AWE for God. Chris Mann was in awe of Christina Aguilera in 2012, and much of the world is in awe of its own views. There is only one who is "the way, truth, and life." His name is Jesus. It is this Jesus that leads us to want to make a difference in a world that knows not Jesus nor honors Jesus.

ONE MUST HAVE FAITH IN THE TRUTH OF GOD.

In this moment of AWE, Jesus laid His right hand on John. Hear Jesus' voice, "Fear not." The one who speaks has perfect knowledge of every event in the past, present, and the future. Jesus was here when the world began. He will be here when the world is no more.

He is the one who is "the eternal living one." He defeated death, and He will live forever and all in whom He gives life will have life forever more. Look closely at the Lord. He is holding the keys of eternity in His right hand.

Jesus calls John to an even deeper AWE. John, you can have faith in me. I have the truth for you. So, let my voice be recorded by you on the pages of what will come to be Scripture. Look my friends, as John is instructed to write about what has already been in the world, about the world now, and about how the world will come to conclusion.

I can almost see John finding a place where he can write. With the voices of waves in the background and maybe the voices of soldiers and slaves around him, there John clearly hears the voice of God.

The hope of the world is only in this voice. This voice is the only voice that can change the world. If you and I are going to make a difference in the world, it is His voice that we must be intimately connected to. Take time this week to listen even closer to His voice.

STUDY QUESTIONS:

1. In this day with so many voices, what should be our criteria for accepting the truth of a voice? Explain your answer.

2. Most of us have been burned by voices. How do we recover from the fallout of believing false voices?

3. What keeps the Christian from hearing the deep and abiding voice of God? Give examples in your answer.

4. How can you help others to clearly rearrange their lives to hear the voice of God?

5. How does the coming just judgment of God give you peace in a world of injustice?

6. Explain why Jesus has the keys to death and Hades.

7. What will it be like for you to see Jesus for the first time?

8. How can we reach this generation with the voice of God? Explain your answer.

CHAPTER FOUR

Losing Sight of the Why

REVELATION 1:20-2:7

"Notwithstanding present difficulties and dangers,
it is to be remembered that this work is not yours
or ours, but the work of God."

Some days just seem to go on and on. At other times it seems as if my days are like I am on a treadmill. I am as busy as can be, but I am still not getting anywhere. Honestly, I wonder after weeks of doing the same things over and over, am I doing what God wants me to do?

In a particularly difficult season of ministry, the great missionary Adoniram Judson all but gave up on his ministry. It was in that moment when his first convert in Burma gave him words of great wisdom: …this work is not yours or ours, but the work of God.

Oh, how we the church in America need to hear this deeply in our hearts and minds! As I write, many churches are struggling just to keep their doors open. Others are locked in battles for power and selfish visions, while the work the church has been called to, goes without any effort in some of the darkest places in our nation.

I see it in the eyes of many believers who are frustrated by what they are not accomplishing in life. The ability to own homes, travel, and accomplish great feats in the world has left believers holding a life resume filled with emptiness and fear. I see fear in those who do not know how to even attempt something different. I also see it and hear it in the voices of a new generation of believers who want to make a difference now.

As I write this chapter, I feel the urgent prompting of God to carry out God's work in these days of urgency. I believe, as you read this book, there is a longing in you to get out of the rat-race of a life that is busy with nothing of eternal value.

As the aged Apostle John found a quiet place on the Island of Patmos (Rev. 1:19) to be alone with God, he was about to write down the Words of God. What he was doing has counted for God's mission for twenty-one hundred years. Jesus' Words, recorded by John, still have as much of an urgent message today, certainly even more so, than at any other time in the history of the church.

As I open my Bible to verse twenty of Chapter one, I want to know what Jesus said. I know His teaching is for my day, and I know what He says is the key to accomplishing our mission of sharing His message with the world. I know if I grasp what He says, I will make a difference in the world for eternity's sake.

As John writes, He is told that the message (letter) is to be sent to seven churches in the region. John MacArthur gives us insight here:

> "These seven churches were chosen because they
> were located in the key cities of the seven postal districts
> into which Asia was divided. They appear in the order

that a messenger, traveling on a great circular road that linked them would travel." (MacArthur, 42)

I wonder, did one messenger come to get John's revelation or did each pastor (identified as the star of each church) come to receive the letter? If it was the pastors, I can see them taking a peek, desperately wanting to know what Jesus found when He investigated their church.

As a pastor of a growing church, I want to know what Jesus says about my church. I want to know what God says about our ministry and our future. It is not always easy to face the truth, but if we are going to make a difference, we must know the truth of where we are as a church.

I am afraid many church leaders have forgotten "the why" of what we do. I see so many who are struggling to keep the doors open instead of storming the gates of hell with the gospel.

Tom Rainer cites a group of pastors who were serving churches that had lost their way. Hear their honest confession: "We have been playing a game called church. We had no idea what we were really supposed to be doing." (Thom Ranier, *Autopsy of a Deceased Church* [Nashville, TN.: B and H Publishing, 2014], 73).

As John finished recording Jesus' revelation, he addressed the first scroll to the Church in Ephesus. This church, a real church in Jesus' day, and representative of the church in every age, was about to hear the result of Jesus' inside investigation of who they were and what they were about.

Jesus reminds the church of His own resume. He is the God who has sovereign authority. He holds the pastors and churches in His hands. He has intimate knowledge of who they are and what their hearts are driving them to do in life. Take a moment and read Revelation 2:1-6 before you proceed with reading further in this chapter.

Have you ever visited this church? I have been to this church. Not the first church at Ephesus, but churches like this church. I confess I have pastored such a church, and I have been an active leader in such a church.

The first church of Ephesus was founded by Paul (Acts 19). He spent three amazing years here (Acts 20). It must have been one of the largest church plants of his day. Church historians believe Timothy pastored here, and after him the Apostle John came to be the pastor. Early church writers tell us that John spent the last three decades of his life as the pastor of the church at Ephesus. It must have been from there that John was taken into captivity and then into exile.

John was writing forty years (have passed since) after Paul founded this church. The city of Ephesus desperately needed the light of the gospel in the midst of its 500,000 people. In this city stood the temple to Artemis. The church of Ephesus was always facing the onslaught of the occult and the pressure of a sinful people.

Notice what Jesus says of this church's ministry. They were laboring hard in and around the church. Times were stressful, but they were hanging in there. They were patient, and they were bold in confronting the evil around them. They refused to accept the teaching of false apostles, and they were not growing weary in doing so.

This would be a church any new seminary graduate would love to have as his first church to pastor. However, a deeper look reveals a problem. Something deep within had gotten out of order in the church.

To be revealed, the previous sentence was hard for me to write because my heart is heavy for a mega church pastor whose ministry has come crashing down. Could it be that something deep within you and me has gotten out of order? Despite all of their work, the church was not getting anywhere. Had the Lord left the church? Or was it something else?

Look closely brothers and sisters, it was the church members in Ephesus who had abandoned Jesus. Yes, they were loving the work, but not the One they were supposed to be representing and serving.

Jesus was complementary to the church. At first, when they received salvation by grace through faith (Ephesians 2:8-9), it was sweet fellowship. They were in love with their Lord. Jesus was Lord of their time, their talents, their treasure, and they existed to do His will in the world. But now they had left Him. Yes, the first church of Ephesus had lost sight of the "why"!

Could it be so simple? Is it true that the success of a local church's ministry is all about loving Jesus correctly? The answer to our urgent question comes from two-thousand years ago, and it comes from heaven in this very second. Jesus says, "Yes."

Brothers and sisters, with urgency I cry out to God, "How do we get back to our first love?"

Oh, how the tears are flowing as I am writing. I see my loving Savior, not turning away from the church but waiting for her to ask how to get back to our first love. In verses four through seven we find Jesus' answer to our urgent question.

EPHESUS REMEMBER WHEN I HAD FIRST PRIORITY.

In those days it was not about the work, it was about the worship that led to the work. In those days it was not about the adventures of faith, but about the awe of the object of their faith. In those days it was not about building an organization, it was about blessing the One who gave us life. In those days the church wanted to make a difference in the world.

EPHESUS FIGURE OUT WHAT HAS REPLACED ME IN YOUR LIFE.

Where did you fall, and why did you fall away from Me? Take time to see the benefit of what you have been doing. Take time to walk the steps back home. This same call is for us today.

EPHESUS CAST ASIDE WHAT REPLACED ME IN YOUR LIFE.

Yes, you must repent for what you have done. You must come to the place where you are broken for your sin, and you must be willing to turn away from it.

EPHESUS COME HOME TO ME TODAY.

When you come home, your intimacy with God will be restored. You will long to get out of bed to meet with the lover of your soul. You will linger in His love, and you will long to worship at His feet. Sunday will be the high day of your week. Each day you will begin with a fresh approach to making a difference in the world.

I can hear Jesus speaking now, "American church, your ministry means nothing if I do not have your hearts."

There is no middle ground here. The words of Jesus sting, "Or else," KJV. Jesus says, I will shut down your church if you do not turn to me. Brothers and sisters, is your church in danger of losing its light? Are you personally in danger of losing your light before the world? Jesus set a timetable for the first church at Ephesus, and I believe He has set a timetable (He alone knows the timetable) for the American church.

History records the church at Ephesus did not return to her first love, and eventually the church ceased to exist. As we end this chapter, I ask, do you need to take Jesus' counsel given to the church? Does the church you attend need to take Jesus' counsel? If so, why wait another second? Turn to Him now! This is urgent! We have no time to waste.

STUDY QUESTIONS:

1. How would you rate your love for Jesus, with ten being the best? How would you rate the love of your church for Jesus with ten being the best? Give support for your answers.

2. What similarities does the American church have to the church at Ephesus?

3. Why do Christians find themselves in spiritual ruts from time to time? Be honest about yours if you are in one.

4. What ministries are you and your church passionate about? Be kind, but honest. How valuable are they to the work of the gospel?

5. List some ways in which pastors get themselves into slumps of faith and even discouraged in ministry.

6. Does the church in America need the message Jesus gave to the church in Ephesus? Give reasons for your answers.

7. How many years have you been a Christ-follower? What have been the most significant seasons of love between you and God? Are you in such a season? Be honest in your responses.

8. How do we get the message of our "why" out to every church in America? Give more than one answer.

CHAPTER FIVE

Tribulation Trail

REVELATION 2:8-11

*"Eighty and six years have I served Christ, nor has
He ever done me any harm. How, then, could I blaspheme my
King who saved Me?....I bless Thee for deeming me worthy of this
day and this hour that I may be among Thy martyrs and drink the
cup of my Lord Jesus Christ."* –Polycarp, Bishop of Smyrna

More and more it seems as if our freedom to worship God is being challenged. Censorship began in the courthouse, and then it moved to the schoolhouse. However, that was not enough, censorship moved into the public square, and now it stands at the very doorsteps of the American church. Brothers and sisters be assured Satan's goal is the total silencing of the New Testament Church in America.

Are my words the words of a fearful pastor who believes our window of opportunity is closing? Actually, the opposite is the case. I believe God is going to open a doorway for the gospel unlike we have never experienced before. Many may label our day as "a time of tribulation," but I believe heaven will label our day as "a time of triumph."

Yes, this is a day of urgency, but not a tragic and fearful urgency. This is an urgent day for the church to awaken and engage in our mission like the church did in the first century. In this chapter I pray you and I hear Jesus' call to walk this tribulation trail for a purpose greater than we realize. Making a difference in the world is costly, but it is worth the cost.

To help us hear this call and to help us embrace the challenge, I want to take you back to our studies in the book of Revelation. The Apostle John has received revelation from Jesus concerning how He will redeem the earth from the brokenness we have been dying in since the fall in Genesis 3.

The original recipients of the revelation were seven first century churches chosen by Jesus to receive it. Today, only one of the cities has survived. It is the city of Smyrna. Today the city is called, "Izmir" and it is located in the nation of Turkey on the coast of the Aegean Sea. As of 2017, there were 4.7 million people living in the city, making it the third largest in Turkey. Since the turn of the twentieth century, the population has become predominately Muslim. Those who follow Christ in this city find it to be a tribulation trail.

In John's day, Smyrna was the second largest city in its country. As we read the words of Jesus directed to the church at Smyrna, we find no words of correction. This church, along with the church at Philadelphia, were the only two churches living fully in obedience to God.

In the second century, the famous church father, Polycarp, would suffer a notable martyrdom as the pastor of this great church. This church was going through a season of ministry Jesus identifies as "tribulation." This tribulation was made worse with the poverty that came with their stand for Jesus. Their Jewish neighbors were slandering them before the Roman authority. Imprisonment would come as a result of Jewish slander.

The church at Smyrna was truly walking on the tribulation trail!

I wonder, as you read this chapter, are you on this same trail? Last week I talked with a Christian brother in our church who said, "Pastor, it is hard to be a Christian in our world." He went on to share his story of facing extreme pressure in his workplace to simply become silent about his faith. I could see the tension on his face. But I also saw the resolve of a brother who would not be silent because of his love for Jesus. He had the resolve that Jesus was directing the church at Smyrna to have.

Let's open this letter Jesus sent to that ancient church. Its words are not only for that church, but also for our church today. No matter what you are facing today, look with confidence at the one who is speaking. John identifies Him as "the one who is first and last, the one who died and came to life," (2:8).

Brothers and sisters see Jesus as our Eternal God who came and endured the greatest tribulation trail of all time. Jesus walked that trail all the way to the cross. In His dying He became our redeemer (Rev 1:7). But death could not hold Jesus. By His resurrection, He became the author of eternal life (Rev 1:18).

It is this God, the one true and living God, who "knows" what His children face. I am so thankful for my Savior who did not retire when He ascended back into heaven (Acts 1:11). Jesus has perfect knowledge about our tribulation trail. Because Jesus has perfect knowledge He knows exactly how to lead His church down the tribulations trails of life.

As I read Jesus' message to the church, I find comfort and challenge in Jesus' words to those on the tribulation trail.

I find comfort and challenge in knowing God knows all about my tribulation.

Take a moment and re-read the previous sentence. Now allow it to sink in. The Lord knows about your tribulation. He knows the trouble you face, and He knows what you are suffering through. He has full identification with you in the afflictions you face standing for Him.

The church in Smyrna had come to "poverty" for their stand on this trail. Because the church worshipped the true and living God, they were not worshipping the officially sanctioned Roman gods. It was natural that they would be forced to quit their jobs.

Jesus says, "even though you are in poverty, you are really rich." The church needed to be reminded of what they had in Christ. James writes, "We are rich in faith." Be assured God will meet your need in this hour of urgency (Phil. 4:19). For many in this generation the challenge is great. Will this generation seek fortune at a cost, or will they seek to make a difference in the world, which also comes with a cost?

To add insult to injury, the Christian church's Jewish neighbors were slandering them before the government. The Jews wanted the church to be persecuted. They, along with Rome, were a part of Satan's church (synagogue). They were opposing God. Be assured you and I are in an urgent war with Satan and his church.

I find comfort and challenge in knowing God is with me on this trail of tribulation.

When Jesus said, "Do not fear," He was not saying they were wimps and they needed to suck it up. The opposite is true. Jesus was saying, I am with you. James Hamilton gives us insight here:

"Tribulation is painful and wearisome. It pecks away at us little by little, chipping away at our joy, taking the wind out of our perseverance, and things only worsen as tribulation drags on." (Hamilton, 77)

Knowing Jesus is with us leads us to stay on the trail. Jesus does not want you to turn from fight to flight in your faith. Our Lord does not want you to become spiritually fatigued because you are constantly in fear. Jesus says, "Peace be still, I am with you." John 16:33

Brothers and sisters, we cannot let the tribulation drive us away from our assignments which are for our good and for His glory. Jesus was very transparent with the church in Smyrna when He said, "It's about to get worse." (Vs: 10)

Suffering was going to intensify. The Devil was going to throw (cast) some of the church members into prison. Now, some who are reading this might be thinking, how does this apply to me; I am not being threatened with imprisonment.

Pay close attention. The word "prison" can also refer to any place where you are guarded, watched, or observed. Brothers and sisters, you and I are living in a day where we are always being watched. Jesus uses the word "testing." The KJV translates the word as "tried."

I find comfort and challenge in knowing God will win the fight if I am faithful to Him.

When we are walking in obedience to God on this tribulation trail, we will be observed as a people who are loving, living, and being a light to those who are in the darkness. It was said of Polycarp, never was a man more filled with light and love as this pastor, than when he was being burned at the stake.

It is true, the world wants you to sin. The world wants you to be like them, but they do not know that their great need is for you to win with Jesus. Brothers and sisters let me challenge you to see your tribulation trail as your time of service in the field of ministry. Let me challenge you to consider the pain you are in as your platform for Christ. The larger your pain - the larger your platform for Jesus will be.

Brothers and sisters let me comfort you in reminding you of the rewards which are coming. You will receive the crown of life. The Lord calls you a conqueror. You will never experience the Second-death which is eternal separation from God (Rev. 20:6, 14; 21:8).

As you travel this week on the tribulation trail, hear the words of Jesus, "Be faithful." Hear them again, "Be faithful." This is our urgent call in these days. The church at Smyrna was faithful, and now it is our time to be faithful in these urgent days.

STUDY QUESTIONS:

1. How has this week's chapter comforted you and challenged you in your faith? Give examples in your answers.

2. Describe the difficulties you hear others facing in their faith.

3. Define what Jesus means by "a synagogue of Satan?" Do we have any such places in the United States? Give examples in your answer.

4. What should the Christian's response be when he or she faces slander? Cite Scripture in your answer.

5. If you were facing death for your faith, do you know how you would respond? Take time to consider your answer.

6. What is the Crown of Life?

7. What is the Second Death?

8. What type of faith does it require before you can be known as a conqueror?

CHAPTER SIX

A Church in a Difficult Place

REVELATION 2:12-17

"America has only two choices: continue on its
ungodly path to destruction or respond to
God's call for repentance." —Bill Bright

There I stood about to speak at a civic function. I had no restrictions given to me as to what my topic was. The group hosting the event was very kind and very much friendly to the gospel. However, the crowd was different. I could sense the animosity, and I could even see it when I was introduced as the Pastor of FBC of Jackson, Georgia.

My flesh whispered, "Keith water it down a little, no one expects you to take a bold stand." The enemy boasted, "They don't want to listen. You are about to get into major trouble."

However, deep within me the Holy Spirit said, "Preach the Word! Be bold when it is popular and when it is not popular. Keith, fulfill your ministry."

As I spoke the living Word of God, the fight was on. It was difficult, and it was at times almost overwhelming, but in the end the Word of God did its work as many lives were changed. Brothers and sisters, you and I live in a day of urgency. It is a day when there is a drying up of Gospel-centered evangelism and Biblical preaching.

Who are the pastors and who are the churches calling for America to repent? In the days before his home-going, the late Bill Bright, founder of Campus Crusade for Christ wrote a book pleading with the American church to stand up to the ungodly path America had chosen. This book was written in 1998. Imagine what Dr. Bright would write if he were alive today.

Brothers and sisters, the church finds itself in a difficult place. The difficultly is far worse than most realize. The church is trying to win the war with the Devil and sin without any weapon of warfare. The Apostle Paul wrote about the church's weapons of warfare in Ephesians 6. One piece of the armor is "the sword of the Spirit, which is the Word of God" (Eph. 6:18).

In Revelation 2, Jesus speaks of His Word as being a "two-edged sword." Simply put, the Word of God is our only offensive weapon to turn the tide of Satan. But consider this. When a pastor and or his church compromises the Word of God, they have dulled the blade on both sides. Even worse is when a church chooses to lead generations into programs instead of the powerful truth of God's Word. If this generation is going to make a difference in the world, they will need to be led to know God's Word.

As the messenger of the Apostle John carries John's written record of Jesus' revelation to the seven churches in Asia, it is as if the messenger has God's two-edged sword in his hand. When the messenger arrives at the church of Ephesus, the Word does its work in reminding the church at Ephesus of their need to restore Jesus to the throne of their hearts. Jesus alone must have first place in their hearts (2:1-7). The messenger's second stop was in Smyrna (2:8-11) where the Word again did its job in encouraging the church with the promise of success in the midst of tribulation.

Now the messenger is making the fifteen-mile journey to the great city of Pergamum. In John's day, this was the capital city of Asia. This had been their position for over 250 years. The city boasted of its worship of many deities. But above all, it boasted of being the first city to build a temple dedicated to emperor worship in honor of Emperor Augustus.

In this city a church had been planted, a church with faithful believers. But now it was becoming difficult to stand for Jesus. John MacArthur helps us understand the difficulty with his commentary:

"Elsewhere in the Roman empire, Christians were primarily only in danger on the one day per year when they were required to offer sacrifices to the emperor, but in Pergamum they were in danger every day." (MacArthur, 85).

Jesus' message to this church stands as a wakeup call to every church to hold fast to the Word of God delivered to the saints. Here before us in this letter we find the great value of the Word of God:

THE WORD OF GOD GIVES
ENCOURAGEMENT TO OUR LIVES

Jesus' Words encourage the church by reminding her of Jesus' presence and His awareness of their difficulty. He commends this church for standing for Him (my Name) in the very place where Satan has a strong hold. The city was filled with idolatry and immorality. But in the midst of its sinfulness, there stood the church as a testimony of God's call to a different life. The church was remaining true to Him. Even when their brother and faithful church member Antipus was killed for his faith, they did not deny their belief in Jesus Christ as their Lord and Savior.

Oh, how they needed this encouragement! The pressure must have been intense. Today the church in many places finds this same type of pressure.

As I write this chapter, an email popped up on my screen from "The Voice of the Martyrs." The headline read, "Christian mother in India stoned to death outside her home for simply giving a neighbor a Bible."

I wonder, what did Antipus do to merit such a death? Did he own a bakery where he refused to make a cake that honored the emperor as God? Did he lose his life because he was hosting a prayer meeting in his home?

Jesus' words were of great encouragement to continue forward in faith. Jesus spoke to His disciples in Matthew 10 with encouraging words:

> "28 And do not fear those who kill the body but cannot kill the soul. Rather fear him who can destroy both soul and body in hell."

THE WORD OF GOD CHALLENGES OUR LIVES

Jesus speaks with a loving and righteous heart when he challenges the church with the things they are failing to do in this wicked city. The church had members who were influencing other members of the church to engage in practices of idolatry and immorality.

Jesus compares their evil to that of the Old Testament false prophet, Balaam, whose story we read in Numbers 22-25. Apparently, there were also those who taught the false doctrine of the Nicolaitans which was in line with the practices of mixing religion and culture. MacArthur comments:

"They believed one could attend pagan feasts, with all their debauchery and sexual immorality, and still join the church to worship Jesus." (MacArthur, 88)

We see this today with many churches being filled with people who have their daily fill of the world system while at the same time boasting of their love for a Holy God. Jesus knew this church was on the brink of following the path of the churches of Thyatira and Sardis. James Hamilton's commentary is revealing:

"The believers seemed to be flirting with evil. They are not openly embracing immorality and idolatry but are not closing the door to it either." (Hamilton, 86) _

THE WORD OF GOD GIVES
US THE WAY BACK TO GOD.

Jesus says, "Repent." Yes, this word gives us the way back to God. But some may say it is a hard word. Brothers and sisters, radical surgery can be hard, but it saves our lives when cancer must come out. Jesus says, "Repent." This word speaks of the change of direction needed by the church.

If the church did not repent, Jesus spoke of the judgment that was to come. His words were as a two-edged-sword that would bring judgment on the church. I read somewhere, "One does not want his or her church to be fighting with Jesus."

When the Lord returns, everyone will know which churches were with God and which were against God. (II Thess. 2:8; Isa. 11:14)

Oh, what promises we read from Jesus to those who obey the Word of God in these difficult days! Jesus promises to give each His life (manna from Heaven). Jesus is the Bread of Life (John 6:35-38). Jesus promises eternal life which is represented by the glorious white diamond stone.

Brothers and sisters think about the joy we will experience when we get home with Jesus. The days of difficulty will be over. It will be peace forevermore. But until then we are called to live as conquerors in this world.

I want to challenge you to pick up the Sword of the Spirit and stand for Jesus. Take the sword with you to work, to school, into the world, and especially with you to church. The world can never choose the path of repentance unless they know what it is.

STUDY QUESTIONS:

1. Consider the white stone as your key, what is the most valued possession in the world?

2. According to Bill Bright, America has two choices before her. In your opinion which choice is she making?

3. In your opinion, list the top 5 false teachings of our day.

4. How would you counsel someone who said, "The Bible needs to be updated"?

5. Describe how difficult it would be to live for God in the city of Pergamum. Name some American cities that compare to Pergamum.

6. How important is it that the church never compromises the Bible?

7. How often do you read the Bible? How often does the Bible form your views concerning life?

8. Make a prayer list of churches, pastors, and places where they need the Word of God. Share your list with a group.

CHAPTER SEVEN

Tolerance

REVELATION 2:18-29

"If churches expect to have anything to say about how Christians do live, they will have to say something about how Christians do not live." –Mark Dever

The pastor stood before his deacon body with a deep burden in his heart. He had previously shared his burden with the deacon chairman. The chairman, after much prayer and meditation, shared his burden.

The deacon body could tell their pastor was broken over something. The pastor began speaking with the following statement: "Brothers we have made a grievous error that I take full responsibility for." The pastor continued, "I know some of you will not understand, but I must tell you, we have not been properly caring for our fellow church members."

One of the deacons spoke up interrupting the pastor. He disagreed with the pastor. "I think we are doing a great job with our deacon family ministry plan. We are not perfect, but we are caring."

The pastor responds, "I am not referring to our deacon family ministry plan. I am referring to the way we are failing to hold accountable those who are living in open rebellion against God." Suddenly the room turned silent.

Pastor Ryan Brower of Cave City Kentucky Baptist Church could identify with the above as he and his church took a bold stand back in 2017 by sending 70 members of their church individual letters challenging them to again begin attending church on a regular basis. *The Lexington Heard Leader* wrongly reported on the incident claiming the Kentucky church kicked out church members over common transgressions.

Question: Was it right for this local church to take so seriously the lack of commitment of its church members? Social media weighed in with a "no" answer and most people joined in condemning this local church.

Brothers and sisters, does the church of the Lord Jesus Christ really need to take seriously all the commands of God? I believe the answer is "yes." I believe the Bible gives witness to this truth. I believe the American church is at a crossroads that demands an urgent return to obeying all the commands of God. This new generation of believers is demanding the truth for their day. If the church is going to make a difference in the world, she must have committed Christ-followers.

As we look back to the early church, we find Jesus' urgent messages to seven churches. To each of these churches there was the call to complete obedience. Two of the seven were walking in obedience. The other five had serious issues because of their lack of desire to obey all the commands of God.

In this chapter we consider the church at Thyatira. Take a moment and read Jesus' letter to this church. Imagine if the church at Thyatira had put to a vote whether the church needed to completely obey the commandments of God. I believe some in the church would have voted against it being necessary to obey every commandment of God. Such members would probably have boasted of the grace of God. I believe many others would have voted for complete obedience to God's commands. I can almost hear them reciting Jesus' words which they had just received from the hand of the Apostle John.

I can almost hear the rebuttal coming from the other side. This side would boast of being a loving church, one that had faith in God, and one that was serving others. This group finishes their rebuttal by saying, they had even patiently endured those in the unions who were pressuring them to quit coming to church.

The church at Thyatira was situated about forty miles north of Pergamum. This city did not have as many false gods as did the other cities, but they did boast of serving the Greek sun god, Apollo. The city was known for its manufacturing of wool and other types of dyed wool. We would say that it was a blue-collar town. The local guilds (unions) ran the city. It was here that the church stood, and it was here where the church had stood for God.

Jesus has told John to send a message to the church. Certainly, we do remember Jesus. He is the Son of God. He is the one who has all authority over His church (Eph. 1:21-23). Take a moment and look into His eyes that He Himself describes as "a flame of fire." He is the all-knowing God who does not tolerate sin, its excuses, and its cover-ups. Jesus is the God who stands firm in His convictions of what is right. Jesus will not compromise even one of His commandments. The church can trust that God never changes.

As Jesus speaks to the church, the church must listen to His address with urgency. Jesus says to the church at Thyatira, you and I are in opposite places - you tolerate a woman identified as Jezebel who is leading people in the church to practice immorality and idolatry. The leaders of the church are allowing this woman to seduce people away from obedience to me (Jesus).

The word immorality comes from the Greek word, "porneusia." The N.L.T. makes the problem so clear, "You are committing sexual sin." This word speaks to any type of sexual activity outside the lines of God's divine design.

This may be new to you, but the Bible has a divine design for all of humanity. God's design is for one man to marry one woman and to live in obedience to him until death does them part (Gen. 2:24-25; Eph. 5:22-31). This is God's design that man chose to walk away from in Genesis 3. When humanity lives according to God's design, it is for following purposes: procreation, pleasure, partnership, protection, and praise to God. Outside of God's design is "porneusia." The Bible calls this "sin."

I can see a church member raising his/her hand and asking to speak. "Jesus, I thought you told us to love everyone. Should we not be tolerant of everyone's opinion and their sexual preferences?"

Erwin Lutzer speaks to this urgent divide in our day:

> "Our culture is being shaped by religious fragmen-
> tation, widespread disaffection with the church, chang-
> ing sexual attitudes, and moral and spiritual relativism.
> Add to this political correctness with tolerance. The
> world is a different place." (Erwin Lutzer, *The Church in
> Babylon* [NEED city, publisher, year], 53)

What should be our answer for this day? Our nation preaches tolerance. I looked up the word tolerance in *Webster's Dictionary* because tolerance means so many different things in our day. The actual definition of tolerance is, "the ability or willingness to tolerate something such as one's opinion." (*Webster's Dictionary*, 2008 edition)

A 2018 edition of <u>Psychology Today</u> cited the difference between tolerance and acceptance. "Acceptance is simply recognizing the reality of a view without attempting to change it or protest against it." "Tolerance, Acceptance, Understanding," *Psychology Today*, 15 Feb 2018

How can Jesus say, this is a wrong view? The answer is clear; He set the standards, not humanity. We are called to obey His commands - not to write, redefine, or establish new commandments. Many churches have failed to hold fast to this truth. Tolerance has become the trap of our day with the end results being the takeover of sin. This is the path tolerance takes.

The church in Thyatira was facing a moment of decision. Jesus gives the church two options. She can repent. He has given the church time already. If she does not repent, judgment was certainly coming, not only to her, but to those who would come behind her.

Brothers and sisters, we need to heed this warning. Jesus has given the American church ample time to repent. Unless we turn around, judgment is already being seen. Churches are losing their influence, and we are in danger of losing entire generations to the enemy.

I am thankful to write that just like some in the church in Thyatira who stayed the course of obedience, many churches are still staying the course today. Many churches have not given into tolerance (identified by Jesus as the deep things of Satan). Such churches are disciplining and discipling their brothers and sisters to obey the commands of God.

Jesus' word to the church of Thyatira was the same word He is giving to us today. We are to "hold fast." We are to be strong in the power of Jesus Christ (I Cor. 15:57-58). We know there is coming a day we will rule and reign with Jesus in heaven. The fight may be hard from here on, but someday we will stand victorious on the field of battle with many of those we would not let go to the enemy. The word of our day is not tolerance, it is truth in Jesus Christ!!! Be assured the truth will set you free.

STUDY QUESTIONS:

1. Define tolerance from God's viewpoint and from the world's viewpoint. Do these viewpoints have any common ground?

2. What are the hot topic issues of tolerance in our day? What does God's Word have to say about the topics you listed?

3. How would you respond if homo-sexual friends invited you to their wedding? Give reasons for your response.

4. How would you respond of a Muslim asked you to attend their worship service? Give reasons for your response.

5. How hard is it to stand for truth in our day? Explain your answer.

6. Jesus says, "Hold fast until I come." How much does it cost to hold fast?

7. What types of idolatry tempt Christians today?

8. What does the Morning Star represent?

CHAPTER EIGHT

The Church that Fell Asleep

REVELATION 3:1-6

"The church can no longer assume the people we are talking to will understand Christian terminology, or why Christians believe the way they do." –Ken Ham

As a boy I used to love to sit near my mother and listen to her either read fairy tales or recite them from memory. One of those stories, written by Washington Irving, was entitled, "Rip Van Winkle."

The story's plot line was simple. Rip Van Winkle lived a life of ease which his wife highly disliked. He was liked by all as a guy who enjoyed life but really did not work nor did his life count for anything significant. After a period of enduring his wife's nagging, he wondered off into the wilderness and ended up drinking a magic potion and sleeping for twenty years. When he awakened, he went back to his city to discover how things had radically changed. It was as if time had passed him by.

The world we live in has radically changed over the last twenty years. There was a day when most Americans claimed to be Christian in their belief system. There was a day when most Americans knew who Jesus is. But that day is no more.

Could it be true that the church has been asleep for the last twenty years? I want to be honest and at the same time compassionate when I say - the church has been busy with programs while the world around us has been indoctrinated at the hands of moral relativism.

Moral relativism is the idea that there is no universal set of moral principles. This is a version of morality that advocates "to each their own." Dr. Ken Ham shares shocking truth for our day:

> "Most churches are not teaching their young people how to defend their faith. Most churches are not teaching apologetics. Because of this, so many kids are growing up doubting, not defending the Bible as the infallible Word of God." (Ken Ham, *Gospel Reset* [Green Forest, Ariz.: Master Books, 2018], 70)

This must become a day of urgency. The church cannot afford to sleep any longer. Even now one generation has been lost to the slumber of compromise. The church cannot afford to sleep any longer. I believe this generation wants to make a difference in the world. But because the Church has failed to theologically prepare this generation, they are trying to discover the answers to questions that the Church has become silent about.

The natural question to ask is: How do we turn it around now? I believe the answer for sleeping churches is found in Jesus' message to the church at Sardis.

The church at Sardis existed in the first century. Today, Ancient Sardis and its ruins are located about sixty miles east of the Izmir Peninsula. The national Turkish travel website advertises the site as:

> "Sitting on the banks of the Pactolus River, it was also one of the seven churches of Asia, mentioned in the New Testament book of Revelation. Called the church that fell asleep, it referred more to the manner of Christian citizens living in the city, rather than the actual church congregation itself."

Did you notice the description above, "the church that fell asleep"? These were Jesus' words to this church in the first century. This was one of the seven churches Jesus directed John to send the letter of Revelation to.

Church historians believe the church had been established by Paul when he was in Ephesus (Acts 19). As we pick up the text, we assume the messenger arrived with the letter. I know I am just speculating, but think with me. I wonder, had the messenger ever been to the city before this trip? This was a thirty-mile journey south of Thyatira. As he approached the city, did he ask for directions to the church? I wonder what people said about the church.

We do not have answers for those questions. However, we do have Jesus' assessment of the church. Jesus said, "the church had a reputation of being alive." The word reputation can be translated as, they had a name around town as being a busy church. James Hamilton believes Jesus is referring to their constant work in keeping the false teachings of Jezebel and the Nicolaitans out of the church.

Here was a church busy with activity but without the uniqueness of a redeemed church. John MacArthur comments:

"Like so many churches today it was defiled by the world, characterized by inward decay, and populated by unredeemed people playing church." (MacArthur, 111)

The church seemed to be very active, but the city no longer heard the gospel from the people in the church. The silence was everywhere in the city. If the church continued in its decline, the doors would eventually close.

Swindoll writes about such churches in his unique way:

"Maybe Jesus' words mean their sanctuary was a morgue with a steeple. Its congregation of corpses with undertakers for ushers, embalmers for elders, and morticians for ministers. Their pastor graduated from a theological cemetery." (Charles Swindoll, *Insights from Revelation* [Grand Rapids, Mich.: Tyndale House Publishers, Inc., 2011], 63)

This may be true of churches today, but for the church at Sardis, this did not seem to be the case. Jesus' words remind us that the church at one time had both "heard and received the Word of God." But now they were no longer standing on the truth.

It seems that the church was busy doing church without God's Spirit. It seems as if the church had bought into a view that said - let's love everyone and try not to offend. Jesus said, you have a name of being alive, but you are dead. It was as if they were ashamed to share their faith with the people in their city. Was there hope for the church?

I believe the answer is clearly yes. But if the church ignored Jesus' message, the church was headed to certain death. This brings me back to a question for our day: Is the church in America done for in the twenty-first century? The answer is absolutely no.

But it could be yes for those congregations who have ceased defending God's Word.

In these verses, Jesus gives a five-fold ministry plan to bring back life to sleeping churches:

WAKE UP

This strong command from Jesus is intended for immediate impact. They were not to make changes slowly. They needed a radical change in the moment. The church was losing the souls of its citizens. Sin had come in, and they were giving in and giving up. It was time to get back in the race with Jesus (I Cor. 15:34).

BUILD ON THE FOUNDATION

The church needed to get back to the Bible. They needed to return to the fundamentals of the faith. They were not meeting the requirements given by God, because they were not in God's Word. The church needed to once again lean on those who had stayed the course in faithfulness to God's Word and not soiled their garments.

REMEMBER WHAT YOU BELIEVED

The church had been established on the foundation of the apostles' doctrine. The church had believed on the Lord Jesus Christ as their Lord and Savior (I John 5:4-13). The church, at one time, had been a strong authentic witness, but now they were on sinking sand. They needed to remember who was really Lord.

START LIVING OUT THE GOSPEL

The church needed to allow Christ to transform them (Romans 12:1-2) instead of allowing culture to transform them. It was time for the church to get back to sharing their witness by their words and their deeds.

REPENT

I know this is a strong command, but here is where it must begin. The church at Sardis needed to do business with God before they could do His business of Kingdom work in the world.

John does not tell us if they repented. However, Church history tells the story of a powerful Bishop from Sardis by the name of Melito who was a strong leader in the church at large. It was he who wrote strongly about the need of the church to be a strong witness in the world. John MacArthur comments, "There was at least some revival that took place in the church," (116).

Now, as we look to our day, twenty-one centuries later, what will we do? I believe the Lord Jesus is challenging us to take those same five steps forward. When we do, we will become a church that again conquers instead of cowering behind the walls of the church.

Brothers and sisters, we are called to make a difference in this world as conquerors. Jesus promises that when we die, He will present us to the Heavenly Father as one of His children. Never let it be said of any church that they went to sleep while their city perished.

God has called us into a day of urgency, and it is a day that counts. Awake all who sleep and repent! Remember what you believed and start living out the gospel.

For all who are awake, your plan is before you. The gospel defended is a gospel that defeats the enemy. The gospel that defeats the enemy is the gospel that delivers souls for eternity.

STUDY QUESTIONS:

1. Why have so many churches closed their doors to the outside world? Give illustrations in your answer.

2. Why is Jesus qualified to judge the church?

3. What areas of death do you see in your local church? Be kind in your answer.

4. What doctrines seem to have been lost in the mainline churches of today?

5. How can you help neighboring churches to come out of their sleep? Give several options.

6. What must a believer do to become a conqueror in our world?

7. Why is it important for Jesus to confess your name before God the Father?

8. What is your church doing to reach its world?

CHAPTER NINE

The Unstoppable Church

REVELATION 3: 7-13

"With broken heart and head bowed low in sadness,
but not in shame, I report to you Mr. President that I must
arrange terms for the surrender of the fortified islands of Malila (Manila)
Bay. Please say to the nation that my troops and I have accomplished all
that is humanly possible..." –General Wainwright citation

On May 9, 1942, all hope was lost for the American forces in the Philippians (Philippines). The day of surrender was a day no one in the American forces could have imagined. But it happened.

On Malila (Manila) Bay there were fifty-four army nurses who wondered what the future would hold. One nurse remembered her thoughts, "Would we be raped, and would we be killed or maybe when the fighting is over things will get better." (Elizabeth Norman, *We Band of Angels* [United States: Random House Publishers, 2013], 131)

As I sit here writing this chapter, I also wonder what the future holds. As I look back over history there have been many wars fought, and there have been many victories and many defeats. There have been many new nations formed and many who ceased to exist.

But there has been one kingdom that has continued to exist, the Kingdom of God. And there has been one institution that has continued to thrive. That institution is the Church. Jesus said, "I will build my church and the gates of hell will not prevail against it." (Matt. 16:18)

The news from around the world is good in many places with the Church thriving and the Church taking the gospel to the people groups who have never heard. But what is the news here in America?

The numbers are staggering. Between 100-200 churches close per week. This is a staggering 1,000-6,000 churches closing every year in America. This begs the question: Has God lost His power? This leads to another question: Has the church fought as faithfully as we should for our future?

God has not lost His power. His Church is still thriving and growing all over the world. Brothers and sisters, this means the second question is where we must look for answers.

With urgency, God is leading many of us who are church leaders to strive to make a difference now. We believe God has a future for the American Church if the American Church returns the ownership of the Church back to God. I believe God is raising up a new generation of Christians who can reclaim this nation for the honor of God. With all of my being I know the church of the Lord Jesus Christ is still unstoppable!

This was part of Jesus' message to the church in the first century. We see one of those unstoppable churches in our focal text for this chapter. This church was Philadelphia. John MacArthur's research helps us to understand the city and the church:

"The church was beautifully situated in the city of Philadelphia which was in a valley about thirty miles from Sardis. The city was given its name after a king by the name of Attalus II who had such love for his brother that they gave him the nickname "brother love." This city endured a major earthquake in A.D. 17, and frequent aftershocks for years to come which left the people living in fear. The church was where it needed to be. Jesus said so." (MacArthur, 120)

This church was unstoppable. But they are not alone in history. There have been multitudes of churches, and there are still churches that have an unstoppable track record. The question is, why? A follow up question is, how can the American Church become an unstoppable Church once again?

The answer is this: We must look to our leader Jesus Christ! Beginning in Vs: 7 we see Jesus and His power. Look closely at Jesus' self-description in this verse. Jesus is the Holy One who is true. He holds the key of David; He opens doors that no one can close; and He opens doors that no one can open.

The church at Philadelphia understood they followed a warrior leader who was Holy God. The church had complete faith in this true God in whom all truth resided. When He spoke, it was the truth. He alone held the keys to Heaven and Hell (Rev 1:18-19). No one could be kept out of Heaven if Jesus opened the door and no one could get into Heaven if Jesus closed the door.

The Jesus they believed in was "The Unstoppable God!"

Churches that believe and follow this Jesus find themselves believing and experiencing three things:

UNSTOPPABLE CHURCHES
LOVE AND FOLLOW HOLY GOD.

When Jesus examined the Church's ministry, He said, "I know your works." This is a wow moment because there is no condemnation for sinful failure or for incomplete work. Certainly, the church was not perfect, but the church was loving and following Holy God.

UNSTOPPABLE CHURCHES
ARE BLESSED WITH OPEN DOORS OF MINISTRY.

The Lord had positioned the church to expand its borders of ministry. Keep in mind when Jesus opens the door, victory is assured for the churches who walk through the door. Now I understand the great opposition in our world today. But at the same time, the opposition is there because it is God's ordained door of opportunity.

Paul prayed for doors of opportunity in Colossians 4:3. Paul knew the enemy of the church wanted to close the doors of opportunity (I Cor. 16:9). Over and over Paul walked through God's open doors (Acts 16:9-11).

UNSTOPPABLE CHURCHES
FOLLOW AN UNSTOPPABLE GOD.

I know the task for this generation of believers seems like a mountain impossible to climb. But this is not the case. The truth is, nothing is impossible for God (Gen. 18:14). The church at Philadelphia had little power. They were a small church without a lot of financial resources but look at the spiritual power that came from heaven. People were being saved, the city was changing, and missionaries were being sent out.

You may be reading this and thinking, what can I do? Please understand, it is God's power that you need. He is the one who is unstoppable. This is the key to making a difference in the world.

The Philadelphia Church kept God's Word, and they have been a witness to all who were around them. The Lord Jesus promised to bring their enemies to their knees. You may today be called intolerable or arrogant or even threatened with regulations. But keep on loving and seeking to liberate people, for God is on your side.

Brothers and sisters, it gets even better. Jesus promises to keep unstoppable churches from the hour of trial. I believe the hour of trial is referring to both times of tribulation throughout history, as well as, to the period of The Great Tribulation. There are others who believe Jesus is making reference to the Rapture of the Church I Thess. 4:13-17). However, there are those who believe, "the church is promised to be preserved through the tribulation." (Hamilton, 116) Either way (Regardless,) the church that follows Jesus is unstoppable.

I wonder, who reading this will be in the number of those who walk by faith through the open doors the Lord has given to His Church. Reword for flow To those who do, the Lord calls out and says, "Conqueror, I am coming." Oh, what good news - that moves us to urgency! When the Lord comes, we will walk through the door of Heaven, and we will have an eternal place there with Him. We will join all those unstoppable church members who have gone before us.

As those 54 army nurses wondered about what the future held, they could only hope they could make it through occupation - with the slight hope that they would be liberated. So, they stuck it out, and hope did come.

Christians have a greater hope. We serve an unstoppable God who cannot be stopped. The question is, who will step forward? Jesus is recruiting conquerors today. Jesus is looking for warriors who will follow Him to the gates of Hell with one mission, to rescue the perishing. Are you ready?

STUDY QUESTIONS:

1. Do you consider your church to be an unstoppable force for God in your city? Explain your answer.

2. How are you directing the next generation to be prepared to make a difference in the world?

3. What do you believe are the greatest oppositions the Church faces in our day? List several for discussion.

4. How would you explain truth to a person who has never heard of God's truth? Give details of your explanation.

5. How should a Christian be praying for the Church in the twenty-first century?

6. What does Jesus mean by "becoming a pillar in the temple of my God?"

7. How does Jesus' statement, "Behold I am coming," motivate you as a Christ-follower?

8. Is God calling you to make a difference in the world? Take time to work through your answer.

CHAPTER TEN

Voices at the Door

REVELATION 3: 14-22

"What should I do with my life? No, what would
God have me do with my life?" – Bill Wallace.

At the age of 17, while working on a car in the family garage, a nagging question haunted Bill Wallace. On that day, July 5, 1925, Bill Wallace made a decision to become a medical missionary in China. Danny Akin writes about his life, "He never looked back or wavered from this commitment," (Danny Akin, *Five Who Changed the World* [Wake Forest, NC. Southeastern Seminary, date], 38)

In a day of urgency, I believe our God is crying out from heaven, "Behold I stand at the door and knock. If anyone hears my voice and opens the door..."

Question, is there anyone reading this book who is on the other side of the door hearing the voice of the Lord? Bill Wallace heard God's voice to take the gospel to China. His efforts penetrated the nation with a gospel that is still bearing fruit in millions of persecuted believers in China.

Today, God is still calling to new generations of people to hear His voice as He cries out at the door of their hearts. This is a day of urgency for the Church because it could be the last age before the Lord returns. It is a day of urgency, because there are more voices of the world system than ever before crying out - come and follow our path. You can have your best life now.

You have a choice today. Which voice will you choose to listen to and follow?

Two-thousand years ago the Church was called into being by the voice of the Living God (Acts 1:18). The Church launched itself into a full-scale mission to reach the world in their generation. As the first century was drawing to a close, there was one more urgent message that came from the Lord. We know this message as the book of Revelation.

God chose to send the message to seven churches. These seven churches had the task of taking the message to the nations. In this chapter we find ourselves arriving with the messenger to the last of the seven cities, the city of Laodicea.

This city was located about 45 miles southeast of Philadelphia. The great Roman road system passed through this city making it an important trade center in what is modern day Turkey. The city was extremely wealthy. They were so wealthy that when their city was severely damaged in A.D. 17 by an earthquake, they built back with their own money. The city boasted of its school of medicine which had developed a power for the cure of eye diseases. Ephaphras was a faithful pastor in this church (Col. 1:7, 4:12-13). The one negative and obvious problem in the city was their lack of clean water. There were impurities in the water system that caused people to get sick. Laodicea received their water supply from two sources. One from the city of Hierapolis which had a hot-water spring and the other from the city of Colossae which possessed a cold-water spring. Laodicea had to pipe the water to the city, but by the time it arrived it was lukewarm.

Jesus' message to this church is strong, and it has much to say for the church in America in the twenty-first century. Jesus addresses this church as the One who is the "amen." He is the One who gives us the facts and says, it is so. He is also the "Faithful and True witness." Anyone can be assured Jesus keeps His Word, and His Word will always be true. He is also "the beginning of God's creation." Jesus was the primary cause of all creation.

Jesus accuses this church of having a spiritual problem. He compares it to the city's water problem. He says, "you are lukewarm." "Luke warmness is being just a little too cold to be hot and just a little too hot to be cold. It's the sin that is probably the most prevalent in the church today." (Adrian Rogers, *Unveiling the End Times in Our Times* [Nashville Tn, Broadman and Holman, 2004], 58))

There was once a person who said to me, "Pastor I am in between churches right now." This person was saying, I am lukewarm. It is the lukewarm church that fails to hear and obey the voice at the door. It is the lukewarm church that has the blight of apathy. Lukewarm churches fail to be God's refreshers in the gospel, and they fail to be healers (in the gospel) for the world around them.

This sin was so great that Jesus said that you are like sickness on my stomach that I have to vomit up. This is a graphic viewpoint given by God. This church, I believe, represents possibly most of the churches in America. We have multitudes of apathetic churches who have gradually lost their love for Jesus. The blight has come slowly. With each new decade, the voice of God calling has gotten weaker and weaker, but not because God's voice is weaker. It is the voices of the messengers that have grown weaker and weaker with compromise and a lack of urgency.

Jesus' voice at the door communicated three things to the first century church and to the Church today:

YOU (CHURCH AT LAODICEA)
SAY, I AM LIVING THE BLESSED LIFE.

The church looked at its financial resources and said, we don't have any needs. The church had prospered, and it seemed that they have forgotten who had prospered them. They believed they needed nothing. Oh, something is wrong with a church that says, there are no needs! While it is true that God has promised to meet all of our personal needs (Matt. 6:33), it is also true that the church I serve stands in great need of all that God offers. We live in a place where 70 percent of the people are without Jesus. We live near a major city in the nation that is as dark as it has ever been. Lord we need your voice today.

I (JESUS) SAY, YOU ARE LIVING
A BLIGHTED LIFE.

This church was not facing facts. They were no longer processing the facts. Someone once wrote, "Any person is a fool who only believes to be true what they write about themselves." The church was now in a spiritually pathetic place with conditions that were pitiful. They were in need of mercy. They had become spiritually destitute.

As I read Jesus' words, I ask, what happened Lord? Jesus' response comes from the Word, "they had become blind." There was some obstruction that had gotten into their eyes. Sin was the obstruction. It was apathy 101.

Question, has something gotten into your eyes spiritually? Could it be that the world now has your ear? The world did not have Bill

Wallace's ear. In 1950, Communist groups began to take over in China and Bill was accused of crimes against the state. He said, "We are what we seem to be. We are doctors and nurses and hospital staff engaged in healing the suffering and sick in the name of Jesus. We are here for no other reason." (Akin, 47). Here was a man who was not living a blighted life.

I believe there are many of you who are hearing the voice of God calling you out of blighted churches, blighted callings, and blighted communities. I want you to know Jesus has so much you want to hear.

I (JESUS) SAY, YOU CAN
LIVE A BETTER LIFE.

Jesus has sweet counsel for us. It is the same counsel He gave Laodicea. They needed to turn away from worthless pursuits of this life and to seek the gold of a life lived for God by faith. The church needed to turn from the black wool of apathetic coverup and turn to the white robes of Christ's righteousness. The church needed to take the salve of the gospel and wipe away the obstructions from their eyes (Eph. 1:18).

This counsel may seem hard, but Jesus tells them why. Jesus was sharing such counsel because He loved them. To all who are in God's family, Jesus is straight forward (rebukes). Be assured God will always expose the blight in the life of His Church. His goal is to remove the blight. But He will only do it for those who want to live a better life.

Be aware, the longer the blight remains the more difficult it is to get the blight off. Jesus counsels the Church to be zealous and repent. With both emotion and energy, the church needed to change directions.

Brothers and sisters, is this the voice you and I need today?

Pay close attention. Do you hear the knock at the door of your heart? Do you figuratively hear the voice of the Lord calling?

- Come to the door which is true repentance.

- Open the door which is surrender to a better life.

- Invite Jesus in which is the beginning of a new life in fellowship with God.

The Bible says, "Jesus will come in and eat with him, and he with God."

I believe there are many of you who have come to the end of this chapter and know the Lord is speaking to you. The Lord has a better life for you. Hear His voice, open the door, and invite Jesus in.

There is much more to accomplish. God intends for you to be a mighty conqueror in this world. Jesus is calling. Embrace the voice and embrace the vision He has for you and for His Church.

STUDY QUESTIONS:

1. Why did Jesus direct the church to be either hot or cold? Could it be that Jesus is asking the church to either side with Him or against Him? Explain your answers.

2. Describe in your own words what it means to be lukewarm.

3. Who are truly the poor among us according to Revelation 3:17? Give reasons for your answer.

4. What is the gold refined in the fire, and what are the white garments mentioned in Revelation 3:18?

5. Does God rebuke every person or are there only certain people God rebukes? Check out Hebrews 12:5-12 as you form your answer.

6. What role does repentance play in the life of a Christ-follower?

7. Why does God stand at the door of our hearts?

8. In what areas of your life is God speaking to you about the need to become a conqueror? Share your answers with the group.

CHAPTER ELEVEN

Changing Your Outlook

REVELATION 4:1-5:14

"When great causes are on the move in the world…
we learn that we are not animals, but people. We know something
is going on in space and time, which, whether we like it or
not, spells 'Duty.'" – Winston Churchill

As I stood at the top of Emperor's View overlooking the city of Zomba, in Malawi Africa, all I could see was the smoke rising from all the fires that had been set by the people on Zomba Mountain. The smoke was so heavy that one could barely stand to be out in it for even a few minutes.

I was not alone in this moment. Missionary Ovi was standing there beside me. I could see the despair written on his face. I knew what was coming next. Ovi asked, "Pastor will we ever be able to make a difference?" He went on to say, "It seems that no matter what we do, things continue as they always have."

In that moment, a strong and powerful missionary for God was ready to throw in the towel. I believe, every great leader faces such moments. It seems that every great move of God in the world comes at a great cost to those who seek to make a difference. The Prime Minister of Great Brittan felt the weight of his day when he was called to do his duty to save the free world from Nazi aggression.

Churchill felt that if his fellow countrymen would do their duty, the world would be saved. Is it true that duty alone leads a person to make a difference in the world? I believe it takes more than duty. Duty often turns into drudgery and ultimately defeat unless there is a cause behind the duty.

Brother Ovi's outlook, even though it was only for a few minutes, had gotten lost in the urgency of the hour. Maybe this is where you are today. Maybe you are doing your duty as a Christian, but if you told the truth, duty has turned into drudgery.

I think there are many churches that find themselves swimming against the current of this day with little gains being made. Many people are saying - it's over, what's the use. Brothers and sisters, the Church needs a change in its outlook. You and I need a change in our outlook.

Before us in Revelation 4 and 5 is an up look that will change our outlook.

Certainly, you remember the book of Revelation. The book of Revelation was written in the last decade of the first century A.D. The last living Apostle of the church is the author. The Apostle's name was John. He was in his nineties when he received a revelation from God. John was living out the sentence of exile on the island of Patmos. It was a Sunday, and John was walking in the Spirit. A voice from behind him spoke (Rev 1:10); the voice instructed John to write a letter to seven churches. John turned to see who was speaking. The voice came from the resurrected Lord of the Church. You know his name as "Jesus."

After a moment to regain composure, John is told by Jesus to write about three different times. First, John was to write about what was taking place in that moment (Revelation 1). Secondly, John was to write about the things that were happening in the churches (Revelation 2-3). Lastly, John was to write about the things that would happen in the last days (Revelation 4-22).

We have already read and written about the first two assignments, and now we are ready to consider the things that will happen in the last days.

Brothers and sisters, we need to see these things so that we can have a change in our outlook.

As John heard Jesus' words in chapter 3 concerning the church at Laodicea, what was happening in the church was discouraging. But now his outlook was about to change. Suddenly as John listens he looks (4:1) upward to the sky and notices a door standing open in heaven!

It must have been a great surprise to John when Jesus invited him through the Holy Spirit to join Him in heaven. We know not how it happened, but the next scene we have is of John describing being in heaven before God's throne. What he saw that day has forever changed my outlook concerning life and the difference we can make in this world.

Notice with me three things about God's throne:

THE WONDER OF
GOD'S THRONE, VS: 1-6A

As John describes the scene, his first priority is the one on the throne. It is God the Father who is sovereign over all the universe (Ps 103:19). "His throne is established in heaven forever." Look with me brothers and sisters at the beauty of the one on the throne. He is described as having the appearance of jasper (diamond) and carnelian (which is a fiery red ruby). This is the best way John knows to describe the glory of God.

John also describes the throne with a rainbow. Hamilton writes: "This is the symbol of God's patient mercy. With justice and mercy in perfect balance, God's glory shines." (Hamilton, 144).

Next, John turns his attention to the 24 elders who are around the throne who are holding angelic court before God's throne. Now we both see and hear the earth-shaking thunder and lightning. We are reminded of Exodus 20 when Israel was afraid to approach the mountain where God met with Moses.

In this moment, I picture the God of beauty also being the God of boldness in justice. In this day that seems to be unfair and unjust, we change our outlook when we know that the God of the universe will one day come and right all wrongs and judge all men with equality and justice (Rev 20:11-14).

THE WORSHIP BEFORE
GOD'S THRONE, VS: 6B-11

Next we read of John's description of four living creatures. John's graphic description helps us to see who God is. Hamilton comments: "God is noble, royal, and fast like a lion. He has a massive, patient, slow, serving strength like an ox. He is sensitive and spirituality that we can see in the face of a human being, and he has a soaring transcendence like an eagle in flight." (Hamilton, 148)

We notice their all-seeing eyes. These four creatures, day in and day out, see God for who He is. They miss nothing. We hear the report of what they see, "Holy, Holy, Holy, is the Lord God almighty."

As I hear those words, I think out loud, finally, someone who is ruling has no skeletons in the closet and has no hidden agenda. This is Holy God. This is the only one who can turn darkness into light.

When these four living creatures give glory to God, all of heaven begins to join them in majestic worship (Vs: 9-11). Brothers and sisters, has your outlook changed yet?

THE WORTH OF
GOD'S THRONE, REVELATION 5

As John continues to write about God's throne we are brought back to the reality of our day. The scene in heaven is wonderful, but how can we make a difference in a world bent on destruction? Dear friend, look back to the throne and notice what John recorded in chapter 5.

John sees the right hand of God the Father. He is holding a scroll in His right hand. One must ask, what is in the scroll? According to Daniel 12:1-4, the scroll contains the Father's will in the redeeming of all things. In other words, the Father held in His hands, His plans for how the world would be brought to its knees before Him and how those who followed Him would be redeemed and how this world would be made new. MacArthur comments: "The scroll contains the title deed to the earth." (MacArthur, 176)

In John's outlook it was impossible for anyone to accomplish such a task. I know this was the weight missionary Ovi was feeling as he could not see how anyone could turn a nation around. Just like John, I wanted to weep in that moment. John knew, if the scroll was not opened, the Bible's promises could not come true.

No one on the earth was worthy (had the power) to accomplish God's plan. But look closer brothers and sisters, because there is one approaching the throne. One of the elders cries out, "The Lion of the Tribe of Judah and the Root of David has conquered."

Brothers and sisters, King Jesus came to this earth as the Lamb of God who took away the sin of the world. The great news is this - He is coming again as King. We see Him at the throne as the crucified Lamb who has risen from the dead.

> "The wounds inflicted on Jesus' body during the trial and crucifixion could still be seen (John 2:24-31). When Christ died on the cross, He defeated the forces of evil. Christ the Lion will one day lead in the battle to finish Satan (Rev. 19:19-21)." *Life Application Commentary, The Book of Revelation* [The Livingstone Corp. 1993]

Do you see Jesus standing there with the scroll? This scroll had the details of how Jesus will execute His reclaiming of what is rightfully His. Jesus has been ready for 2000 years to open the scroll. I believe it may be possible that even now Jesus has his hand firmly placed over the first seal and is ready to break it unleashing the Great Tribulation. Then the end will come.

Brothers and sisters, has this changed your perspective? It has for me. I look beyond the sorrow of this moment knowing King Jesus can change anyone if they will bow before Him. I look beyond the strong-holds of the enemy knowing there will be a day when he will have to let go of his hold on the earth. I look beyond the sin that so easily ensnares the world. When Jesus comes to sit on the throne, all evil will be no more.

Brothers and sisters let us gain a different viewpoint knowing Jesus is redeeming people and Jesus is preparing to return. Let us be about the business of sharing this good news, because it is bearing fruit in the world.

STUDY QUESTIONS:

1. Describe your personal outlook toward the future before you read this chapter.

2. What is the outlook of most people who claim Christ as their Lord and Savior?

3. Write down what you think heaven looks like.

4. Write down what you think God the Father and God the Son look like?

5. What does Jesus mean to you? Attempt to write a song for your response.

6. What is the significance of the Lamb being slain now standing?

7. Describe how the Church would change if everyone truly fell down and worshipped Jesus?

8. Describe your personal outlook toward the future now that you have read this chapter.

CHAPTER TWELVE

A Shifting Culture

REVELATION 6

"The battle degenerated into a butchery and a confused
melee of personal conflicts. I saw numbers of men kill each
other with bayonets and the butts of muskets. And even bite each
other's throats and ears and noses, rolling on the ground like beasts."
—Confederate Officers report at the end of the Civil War

The days of the Civil war (1861-1865) were some of the most wicked days of our nation's history. A few years ago, I spent one summer reading for leisure about the Civil War. The first-hand accounts of the last days of the Civil War made a deep impression on me. I was struck by how our nation had lost its decency for the respect of human life. The desperation of the Confederate army led to their acting like animals in their attempt to simply survive. At the same time the desire for victory led the Union army into the same wicked battles using the same wicked tactics. So goes a people when culture shifts.

I wonder, does anyone see a shift in our culture today? One would have to be totally blind not to see the shift in our culture. Over two-thousand years ago Jesus said, "In the last days... lawlessness will be increased, the love of many will grow cold" (Matthew 24:13). A few verses later Jesus predicted, "Only for the sake of the elect will those days be cut short" (Matthew 24:22).

It would seem that Jesus was predicting a time when not just our nation, but all nations of the world will conduct themselves even worse than those who fought in those last days of the Civil War. It bears mentioning that a people who know beforehand of such a time would do their best to avert such a time and do their best to have their families prepared for such a time.

I believe the cry of God for urgency in our day is greater than at any time in the history of the Church. But many people have become engaged in the battles of this age. We see many who claim Christ who have shifted with the culture. Those who have not shifted have decided to stay away from culture.

Where are you in your efforts to effect culture? The Confederate officer who wrote about the last days of the battle did his best to stop the battle knowing that Robert E. Lee had already surrendered. But his voice fell on deaf and desperate ears. It is my prayer that you, the reader, would have ears that want to hear and a mind and heart that is urgently seeking to reach a shifting culture.

Take your Bible and open to our reading for this chapter. It is Revelation 6. In chapters 4 and 5 we were greatly encouraged by what John saw in heaven. As we left off in our reading, Jesus is standing before the throne holding a scroll. The host of heaven is worshipping at the throne because Jesus has taken the scroll which contained the details of how God intended for the world to be brought to its knees before Him and how the world would be made new.

Do you see Jesus standing there with the scroll in his hands? John sees Jesus opening the first seal that allows us to see the first step in the process of God's redemption through judgment. The first wave of God's judgment begins to be unleashed.

As a side note, I want you to know that I believe from this point forward the writing in Revelation is happening in cycles and not necessarily in chronological order. It seems as if the judgments are happening one after another. The vision of God's judgements gets worse as we walk through these next chapters culminating in chapter 16 at the Battle of Armageddon.

As we look at this chapter, it is the first wave of judgments called the seal judgments. It will be followed by the second wave of judgments called the trumpet judgments. The last wave of judgments will be the bowl judgments.

As John stood there watching and recording what he saw, one of the living creatures called out, "Come." As a Christ follower I am so thankful for this word. It is the word that describes for me the invitation Jesus gave to me on the day of my salvation. Jesus spoke this word in Matthew 11:28 when He said, "Come unto me all you who are heavy laden (burdened down), and I will give you rest." As you read this chapter, know God is still calling people to come to Him through His Son Jesus Christ.

However, on that day, when it comes, there is no invitation for salvation. (However, when that day comes, there will be no invitation for salvation.) This is an invitation to understand the judgment that is coming on the earth. This drives me to a deep urgency for my fellow man.

In rapid succession the judgments of God are released. We see this illustrated by John's description of four horses and their riders. I propose that you not to get caught up in the imagery but in the truth being taught. To help us understand the judgments I have placed them under two headings:

GOD'S HAND BEING
REMOVED FROM SOCIETY

The God of creation (Genesis 1:1), who has been restraining His wrath since the fall, is now ready to release judgment on the earth. I believe these 4 horses reveal how God simply takes His hand off of society and allows man to be his own guide (II Thess. 2:7-8).

Adrian Rogers comments:

> "Some believe it is Christ who is doing all of this. But there is a way the judge can do this that is often overlooked, 'I believe the judge allows the chips to fall where they may and allows the consequences of one's behavior to serve as judgment.' " (Rogers, 85)
>
> In other words, God allows the culture to shift into a lawless state where people lose all morality. In such a culture people strip each other of dignity, they step on each other in order to survive, and they stand against the very God who tried to redeem them.

We see the first horse coming. It is a white horse that represents a conqueror who is coming, but wait he has a bow but no arrow. This must be a leader who is able to conquer by diplomacy and deception.

1. We see a shifting culture being taken in by
a leader who promises peace.

The Prophet Daniel predicts such a time on the earth (Dan. 9:24-27). This leader is described in the Bible as the Antichrist. God allows this leader to rise to power. The world buys into his deception (II Thess 2:9-11).

John 10:10 "The thief comes to rob, steal, and destroy…" John 5:43 "I have come in my Father's name, yet you don't accept me. If someone else comes you will accept him."

Could it be that our world is ripe for such a time as this? Let's just take one city in America. The city of Chicago. There were 42 people shot in the city over Memorial Day weekend, 2019. In a 2014 study, "News Wars" magazine research revealed, there were 60 countries at war and over 492 separatists' groups who were vowing to take over the world.

In a shifting society people bow to the feet of anyone who promises riches without responsibility, wealth without work, and self-gratification without self-investment.

For three plus years there will seem to be peace, but there is another rider being summoned from heaven.

2. We see a shifting culture being taken over by a one world government.

Suddenly in the middle of the Tribulation Period, this seemingly giver of peace (II Thess. 2:4) will break the peace and demand the world to bow before him. Now the peace is over, and the world is at war. Men will now devour each other more than at any time in history.

I believe the type of warfare predicted here will make the holocaust, the genocide in Syria, Civil War in Rwanda, and all the Word Wars look insignificant in comparison to this day that is still to come.

3. We see a shifting culture facing the greatest economic crisis of all time.

As the third horse comes, we see the obvious color of black signifying the darkness of the time. Here we see imagery of scales that are weighing grain out at a price. Swindoll's comments shed light here:

"The measuring scales and the voice shouting prices indicate that this period of time will be characterized by economic inflation and starvation. The prices listed here are about 8 to 16 times the average prices in the Roman Empire at that time... the people will be able to only buy limited amounts of food." (Swindoll, 110)

I cannot imagine the pain of this day. Matt. 24:19 "Woe to women who are nursing in that day."

4. We see a shifting culture burying its dead as the earth no longer provides for its needs.

Brothers and sisters, before we can catch our spiritual breaths, here comes horse number four with a pale color resembling the color of a pale green color that is the color of death upon men and women. One author compared this color to that of a decomposing body.

Now, humanity has sunk even lower. Could it be that men are committing cannibalism? Could it be that now disease becomes beyond our ability to treat? The food that much of the world has wasted on themselves in the past is no longer available. Animals carrying disease pass it on to humanity. I wonder, is the world shifting for the better. I think not.

In this moment, Jesus opens the fifth seal. We no longer see a horse, but we see the souls of slain believers who died for their stand for Christ. Their cry is valid, "God when will you judge the unrighteous of the earth?" Be assured, a shifting world will not leave the Church to live for Jesus.

"These souls are the ones who are rightly related to God and to other human beings. They are slain by people who are doing wrong. They are murdered for fulfilling the two greatest commandments-loving God and loving people. These people are asking that God's goodness be vindicated. Listen to the words of Paul, 'Beloved, never avenge yourselves, but leave it to the wrath of God, for it is written, 'Vengeance is mine. I will repay.' This passage teaches me that this could be you, my children, your children, or me. We need to be reminded to be faithful to the end. The Lord will repay." Cited from (Hamilton, 182-183)

GOD'S HAND BEING REJECTED BY SOCIETY

Now we arrive at the sixth seal. Suddenly the earth that men lived upon and thought they ruled takes vengeance against its people. This natural disturbance of nature is no accident. Scientists tell us that a nuclear war could set off earthquake actions that would hurl so much debris into the air that it would almost blot out the sun. This is depicted in Zechariah 14:12-13.

As Christ followers you and I think, "turn to God now," but a lost and dying world sees no answer in God. They consider God as only their enemy. In this moment in the future He has come to be their judge. No one can stand against this God (Luke 21:36).

As we come to the end of the chapter, I find myself moved, not to despair, but to determination. An even greater urgency is stirred in my heart to make a difference now. I know God is still drawing people to Himself. But that day will end. You and I only have this moment, so let us meet this shifting culture at the cross-roads of life and cry out, "Come to Jesus."

STUDY QUESTIONS:

1. What percentage of the world has never heard of the coming judgment of God? Give proof with your answer.

2. List several illustrations of the shifting you see in society today.

3. Why is it so hard for people to talk about prophecy?

4. How does the future lead you to prepare your family in the present?

5. Who are the world leaders in our day, and how are they influencing our day?

6. Why do people want to follow leaders who promise something for nothing?

7. How should the Church live out their faith in a shifting society?

8. What things have you been challenged to do because of this study?

CHAPTER THIRTEEN

Easter, The Answer for All Your Fears
REVELATION 7

"When you get to where you are going, where will you be?"
—Adrian Rogers

Twelve people got up and went to work on May 31, 2019 as they had many other days. Little did they know that this would be the last day of their lives on the earth. Not one of the city employees of Virginia Beach had any clue that one of their fellow workers had been so disgruntled that he (Dwayne Craddock) would enter the municipal building of the city and randomly take the lives of twelve people.

Sadly, these stories are becoming more and more a regular part of our world. A mother commented to another mother, "There is nowhere to be safe these days. I am always in fear when my children leave our home." But wait a minute, there are many homes where it is not safe to live. The Bible teaches us that the world is going to get worse and worse before Jesus returns (II Tim. 3:3).

The world Jesus entered over 2000 years ago was filled with violence and hatred. Rome was violently in charge of the world. When the religious leaders wanted to kill Jesus, they knew the Romans had the best way to accomplish the task. Crucifixion was a popular method of dispatching threats to the empire. "Romans practiced both random and intentional violence against populations they had conquered, killing tens of thousands by crucifixion," says New Testament scholar Hal Taussig, who is with the Union Theological Seminary in New York.

Jesus came to die so you and I could live. In John 10:10 we read the following: "The thief comes only to steal and kill and destroy. I came that they may have life and have it abundantly." The life we are called to is a life that is free from sin's hold, Satan's harassment, and society's hurts. Jesus came that we would no longer have to live in fear. God's perfect love for us casts out fear (I John 4:18).

It is not fear that drives us to urgency, but a passion to reach this world before it is too late. As we come to Revelation seven it is with an understanding that this world system is headed to both earthly and eternal destruction. In 1 John 2:17, John wrote: "The world is passing away, the lusts thereof, but he who does the will of God will abide forever."

Unlike the world we (Christians) do not have to fear what is ahead. Here before us in Revelation seven are two scenes. One is the scene of God setting apart the Jewish nation for a work still to come, and the other is the scene once that work is completed. Both of these scenes lead us to understand, Jesus is the answer to our fear.

Let's examine both scenes separately, and then we will draw two conclusions:

SCENE ONE:
GOD SETS APART THE JEWISH NATION
FOR A WORK STILL TO COME, 7:1-8.

Keep in mind that I am teaching this from a settled viewpoint that the book of Revelation is not a total chronological order of events. I believe we see cycles of events. For example, I believe chapters 6, 8-9, 15-16 happen one after another (in cycle). I believe chapters 7, 10-11, are placed where they are in the text to give us encouragement to not fear the cycles of judgments that are coming. Having written this, I believe this chapter gives us the first scene just before God unleashes the Great Tribulation.

Chuck Swindoll comments:

> "The staggering scene at the end of the sixth seal ends with people all over the earth rushing to caves and screaming. Those panicked screams echoed in the distance as Christ's thumb lingered at the seventh seal of the scroll." (Swindoll, 117)

As the people cry out, "Who can stand in this great day of wrath," we find the answer in chapter 7. The people who will stand are those who used to stand (for God) but have for centuries rejected Jesus Christ. These are God's people, the nation of Israel. God called them into being in Genesis 12. God promised Israel that He would make them a great nation, and that they would inherit the earth. Brothers and sisters, God keeps His promises. Israel turned away and a partial hardening came upon the people (Romans 11:25). This hardening will continue until the full number of Gentiles come into God's family. Then God's promise will be fulfilled (Romans 11:26-27). The Lord will come and remove ungodliness from Israel (Isa. 27:9).

Now there is much debate about whether this is just Israel or also the complete number of God's people being that 12 sets of 12,000 point to a complete number. I believe God has special work for His people during those days to come.

Here is what He is doing with them:

- God is protecting them as He protected them in the land of Egypt.

The living creatures are told to hold back the winds of judgment (Jer. 49:36; Dan. 7:2) until His people are positioned to work, and I believe all along the way these flaming evangelists for Jesus will be protected just like God protected His people when the plagues where coming against Egypt (Ex. 9:6-7).

- God is setting them apart for the mighty work of reaching people in the last days.

This sealing by God has so many implications. They have been set aside (sealed) and delivered from the wrath to come. Be assured, as Hamilton writes: "The world is not spinning out of control. God is in absolute control of everything that happens." (Hamilton, 189) These have been sealed with the power of the Holy Spirit (Eph. 1:13) to preach and teach the Word of God. They have power to live the Christian life in the toughest of days when eventually following Christ means certain death. Every second of those days before the Lord returns will count.

Now whether these are only Jews, or they represent Jews and Gentiles, you will have to decide. I have decided that I am preparing my family and all I know to be prepared to minister in the toughest of days knowing that persecution and tribulation gives the Christ-follower the greatest platform for truth.

SCENE TWO:
GOD SHOWS US THE SCENE IN HEAVEN, ONCE THE GREAT TRIBULATION IS COMPLETED, 7:9-17.

I believe the Lord is now giving us a view of Heaven after the Second Coming of the Lord in Rev.19:11-21.

People from every tribe and nation will be joined together. So great is the number that no person can count the number of people. But be assured our names are written down in Heaven's record. I try my best to imagine the scene as the people there are all Christ-followers who have been redeemed by the blood of Jesus Christ. It is He who clothes all His people in white picturing having cleansed them all from their sin (I John 1:7).

I see the people, and I see the celebration. I see people waving palm branches reminding us of the days of old when the nation of Israel celebrated the Festival of Booths which reminded them of God's deliverance from Egypt (Lev. 23:40). Hear the shouts of praise to our God who has delivered us from the bondage of sin and from the wrath of the Father. I see God on the throne with His Son (the Lamb) standing by the throne.

Next we see all the hosts of heaven bowing before this great and glorious God, giving praise to His name. Question, who is in the crowd? An even more important question: Will you be in the crowd? There is only one way to be sure that you are in the crowd: Surrender your life to Jesus today.

It is in this moment when even the slightest fear of the future should be put to rest. As God's people, we know where we are headed, and we know where we will be when we get there. There is so much here, but for our chapter I want to offer you two conclusions:

CHRISTIANS DO NOT HAVE TO FEAR BECAUSE GOD KEEPS HIS PROMISES.

There are over thirty-thousand promises in the Bible, and God keeps every one of them. Never once has God lied or will He ever lie. This day, you can say with the multitudes in Heaven, "Blessing and honor belong to our God forever and ever!" In verses 25-27 God gives us five promises. This is a virtual catalog of Biblical promises. God promises to "Shelter us with His presence." In this life God spreads His tent of love and protection over our lives. God promises that we will "Hunger no more." God promises us that we will "Thirst no more." God promises us that the "Sun shall not strike us."

I love these promises. The enemy no longer can hold anything over the Child of God. All of His fear tactics have been removed. All of these promises will happen because the Lamb is in the midst of the throne. Fear no more Child of God. The Lamb has prevailed.

CHRISTIANS DO NOT HAVE NOT TIME TO FEAR BECAUSE GOD FILLS US WITH PRAISES.

When I praise the Lord, my fear meter goes down and my courage meter goes up. Now I find myself being courageous in reaching out to others in the midst of this tribulation world. I do not have to fear, because I know where I am going, and I know He has made the way clear for me.

All of this will take place because Jesus went to the cross, paid the price for my sins, and arose from the grave victoriously. Today, this moment, allow the God of Easter to become your God bringing you out of the grave called fear.

STUDY QUESTIONS:

1. In your studies, who are the 144,000? Give reasons for your answer.

2. Has God given you (if you are a Christ-follower) everything you need to live successfully here? Explain your answer.

3. How does the sealing of God through the Holy Spirit work in the Christ-follower's life?

4. If you know you are headed to heaven, why do you struggle from time to time with fear?

5. Why does God allow the Christ-follower to suffer in this life? Use I Peter 1:8-9 as part of your reasoning process.

6. What does God mean by sheltering us with His presence?

7. What does God mean by promising that we will no longer hunger or thirst?

8. How does the sun strike us in the world each day?

CHAPTER FOURTEEN

Fire on the Earth

REVELATION 8-9

*"As I walked toward the bomb shelter, my mind was
not prepared for what I was about to encounter. The cries coming
from the shelter sounded like wounded animals. The smell caused
me to want to throw up and then I saw them..."*

Winston Churchill was doing a masterful job of covering up the real devastation in his country during WWII. He did his best to make sure there was little said, written, or broadcast about the many people who had been either killed or displaced from their homes because of the devastation of the night bombings. He believed the nation could not afford to be discouraged any farther.

So, there were places hidden away where those who lost their homes went. There were shelters tucked away that were almost unlivable. But compared to the state of the world during the last days of the Great Tribulation, there's was an easy road.

As the cycles of judgment continue to be unleashed on the world in the Great Tribulation, I want to remind you that the people of God are attempting to continue forward sharing the everlasting Gospel (14:5-6) with a world that is facing a day of judgment that is still to come.

Unlike Great Britain, which knew there was hope beyond their destruction, the world of the Great Tribulation has no hope of recovery because the world system devoted to the destruction of and dethroning of God is about to be destroyed. Only those who come to know Jesus as Lord and Savior will make it beyond these days. Some may say, God is unfair to treat the world in this manner.

Consider this. It was not, and still is not, God's desire for the world to be destroyed. God the Father sent Jesus so that the world could be saved (I Timothy 2:3-5; II Peter 3:9). The world continues to want its way, not knowing that it is following the prince of this world. This world system has entrapped those who willingly believe in its system of rebellion. In John's vision, judgment day has come. The fire is falling from heaven.

In chapter eight, John continues to write about the cycle of God's judgements. God's hand of grace has been removed, and the world is on its own. We see heaven's love for the world in the silence that comes when Jesus opens the seventh seal (8:1). This is a solemn moment for heaven and earth. This is the calm before the storm of fire that falls from heaven.

As God's people seek the face of God, the angel of God, following divine orders, takes a censer and fills it with fire and casts it to the earth. It's as if the spiritual B-52 Bombers are headed for their target, which is the earth.

In heaven there are seven angels standing with Trumpets. In the book of Numbers, chapter ten, the nation of Israel knew when the trumpets blew it was a warning for the war that was coming. Paul wrote about the trumpet sounding in I Thessalonians 4:13-18. Brothers and sisters, I look forward to the day of Jesus' return, but at the same time, I do not want to see this day, I do not want to think about this day, but I know it is coming.

As John experiences the silence (8:1), suddenly the trumpet blows. Oh no, the first trumpet sounds: The earth was scorched with fire that damaged what clean air was left in the world. If the smog in Los Angeles seems bad, imagine it one-hundred times worse. Those with breathing problems have no hope of survival. As the people are coughing and searching for clean air, the second trumpet sounds.

Now all the fishing industry loses a third of its resources, and the shipping industry is brought to a standstill. The world that depends on the sea now finds the sea to no longer be of help. The great ports of the world are now at a stand-still. Precious life-saving cargo is at the bottom of the sea or stuck in ports. The world is coming to its knees.

But there is more fire, the third trumpet sounds: the fresh water of the earth is polluted by worm wood. Now there is no answer for the disease that comes as people from all over the earth die from the pollution. Imagine the dysentery and death all around. I have seen this in places of the world, where people never take notice. The world will take notice when the trumpet sounds. A world at war with God's creation is now paying the price as a society that has for centuries abused what was given into its charge.

Could there be more? Do you hear the fourth trumpet sounding? Now the solar system which gives light, health, and growth to all things is cut by a third. The eco system of the world is now out of balance. People are starving and freezing in places where they never have before. Still other places are burning up from record high temperatures. The world seems to be spinning out of control.

Brothers and sisters, no one in their right mind would want to face the fires of judgment. The late Adrian Rogers once said, "I would not wait 15 seconds to come to Jesus, there is too much at stake." I would add, I would not wait 15 seconds without pleading with my family to come to Jesus.

Does this prophecy move you to urgency? Hear the words spoken by the eagle from heaven, "Woe to those who dwell on the earth." There are three more trumpets to go. Yes, you read the previous sentence correctly, there are three more trumpets to go. Suddenly we hear the fifth trumpet sound.

Oh no, it cannot be. What is happening? God releases those things that He has kept in chains since the fall. So devastating is the pain inflicted that people will want to die, and they cannot. It is in this moment I have to ask, why would anyone stand with a world system that has such a future ahead? The power of darkness is great (II Corinthians 4:4-6).

This living hell lasts for five months. It is only a foreshadowing of the hell to come. Hell will not last for only five months. Hell will be forever and ever with the fires of God's judgment. Could it possibly get any worse?

Friend, the worst has not come yet. Suddenly the sixth trumpet sounds. The four creatures bound by God with their mighty army are released. They are not released against the people of God, but against their own people - who stand against the armies of God. Hell has no loyalty. Their evil deeds remind us of their leader, Satan, who is a murderer (John 8:44). All who follow Satan will experience the fires of hell.

Surely the fire will change such people, but wait - it does not change them. Here is truth for our day: If the gospel does not change a heart, fire will not either. This is why, before the fire falls, we must go after the souls of all men.

This is why we must not cover up the truth of the wrath to come. Yes, the gospel is wonderful for all who say, yes to Jesus. But at the same time the gospel is the story of wrath to come for all who reject Jesus. Brothers and sisters be ready. The fire could fall any day now.

STUDY QUESTIONS:

1. What impact will trumpet judgment number one have on our world?

2. Describe what trumpet judgment number two looks like.

3. Why is water so important to our existences?

4. What are the locusts? Are they literal locusts, or do they represent something else?

5. What keeps the people from dying in trumpet judgment number five?

6. Why does the threat of judgment not move most of the world?

7. Why do we love our sin so much at the cost of so much? Reword for flow

8. How close is the end of the world? Are you ready for the end?

CHAPTER FIFTEEN

Urgent Spiritual Updates

REVELATION 10

During World War II, Winston Churchill received daily updates from the battlefield. Each of these updates were crucial to the success and failure of the war. With these updates in hand, the commanders could make the changes they needed in strategy to both strengthen the line against the enemy's attacks as well as plan their offensives against the enemy.

In war, leaders need updates. Updates are also crucial when a major storm is approaching. Most who are going to be in the eye of the storm cling to every urgent update they can receive.

The Apostle John needed (I believe) a spiritual update. He already knew the world was facing a coming storm called "The Great Tribulation." Jesus had said "Look to the skies" (Matt. 12:38-42; 24:25-31.)

John had looked to the skies (Rev. 4:1) and had seen the world self-destructing in the Seal Judgments. He had seen the vision of the Trumpet Judgments. In this moment, John must have been emotionally drained. John must have been wondering when these things would come to be.

As we come to chapter 10, we come to a moment of a break in the cycles of judgment. It's not that the judgments are stopped, but that John needed an urgent spiritual update so that he could continue with confidence to write the updates we need in these days we live in.

As a Christ-follower, I believe we are getting closer and closer to God's return. Jesus said, "Lift up your heads for your redemption is drawing near" (Luke 21:28). The God who redeemed a people for Himself (Colossians 1:14) is coming to rescue us in the days of tribulation.

Think for a moment how wearisome life can become. Consider the single mother who has three children and one of those is a special needs child. Each day she works to provide for these children and then finds out that the government wants her to stay at home all the time with her special need's child. How can she possibly do both?

Consider the kid who wants to get out of the gutter, but the reputation he carries simply because he is from "the bottoms" keeps others from even giving him a chance in life. How can he possibly get a job to earn money for college or even earn money to attend a trade school? What is he to do?

Consider the mom and dad that love their child but live in an impoverished third-world country. Their youngest child has said, "I want to be a doctor so I can save lives." This family cannot even afford a second set of clothes. What will they do?

Brothers and sisters, there are many storms in life. The Devil does his best to make sure the urgent updates from God never reach those they were intended for. However, God is greater than our enemy. In Revelation 10, the urgent update comes to John.

I love the way John begins, "Then I saw…" These words are refreshing to me. They are like fresh water in the November desert of Malawi.

They are like a fresh wind blowing on a hot fall day in South Georgia.

John sees a mighty angel whose description reminds us of the glory of God. A closer look reveals this to be Jesus (1:7). This glorious God is bringing to John an urgent update. This update is written on a scroll. There is much debate as to what was written on the scroll. It is enough to know that what was written brought the needed refreshment to John. In the same way you and I have the perfect word given to us (II Peter 1:19-21), it is our refreshment, and it is our roadmap for every storm.

The one who brings this update (Jesus) is seen placing one foot on the sea and the other on the land. Adrian Rogers comments:

> "In Bible times, when a conqueror overthrew a nation and occupied a piece of land that had a shoreline, he would put one foot in the water and another foot on the land and raise his hand in victory. This gesture meant he had conquered the area. This gesture reminds us that every drop of water and every grain of sand belongs to Him." (Rogers, 128)

In this moment John hears what is written in the scroll, and he is about to record it for us, but Jesus says, "Don't write this down." Brothers and sisters, I believe there are some things that are coming that are better left unknown. I believe the horror the world will face is beyond description.

Jesus says, "There will be no more delay." Brothers and sisters, there will be no more grace. The storms of tribulation cannot be diverted or held back to a later date. It will be time. When the first seal is opened, the wave of judgments is coming and no man, beast, or Satan himself can stop what is about to happen.

One might ask at this point; how can this be a refreshing moment for anyone? I believe the answer lies in which side you are on. If you are on God's side, you know victory is within the gate. But if you are on the enemy's side, you had better change sides.

For those on God's side, this chapter is the urgent update we need. There are no less than two encouraging observations in Revelation 10:

JOHN WAS BEING REMINDED
THAT GOD WAS IN CHARGE OF ALL TIME.

As Jesus continued to speak, He assured John and assures us that He is truthful. There was no one greater to swear by than Himself. We are reminded of Hebrews 6:13, where God promises to keep His own Word. "In essence God said, 'If I don't keep my word, I will cease to be God. By my very existence these things will come to pass.'"

When you and I see the weather forecasts, the Meteorologists always cover themselves by saying, "30, 60, or maybe 90% chance of…" In this way, if it doesn't rain, we cannot label them as false prophets. Here is the good news, Jesus has never been wrong once in the history of the world. He speaks truth, and deeper still, He is truth.

Everything that happens, happens in God's timetable. God is working all things for His good (Romans 8:28-29). You and I need His urgent message to remind us that He is in charge.

JOHN WAS BEING REFRESHED
BY THE GOD WHO WAS IN CHARGE OF ALL TIME.

John is instructed, beginning in verse eight, to take the scroll and eat it. The scroll, I believe, was the Word of God. To eat speaks of consuming or understanding its content. At first the message would be as sweet as honey because of what was going to happen for all who were on God's side. But then it would become bitter because of all that was going to happen to those who were on the Devil's side.

I totally understand this moment because as a pastor and preacher of the gospel, I love His Word, but at the same time my heart aches because of the judgment that is coming to all who reject Him. My heart aches for them, and my heart aches for God, because of all who reject His love and His lordship.

John so needed this urgent message from heaven. John had more work to accomplish, and that work consisted of getting the gospel to all people, all nations, all languages, and all thrones.

Two-thousand years have passed since this urgent message was delivered to John. Now the urgent message has come to you and me. Will you receive His message? Will you allow it to reach you if you are not on God's team? Will you allow this message to recharge you for the journey if you are on God's team? Finally, will you share this message with others in order to reach them with the gospel?

I hope you will be changed today and forever by the urgent message from heaven!

STUDY QUESTIONS:

1. What type of messages get people's attention today?

2. Why doesn't the message of the gospel seem urgent to so many people?

3. In your own words, describe the angel in verses 1-3 of this chapter.

4. What must have been contained in the message that John was told not to reveal to us?

5. How differently would you do ministry if you knew the world only had three more days left?

6. Why was it important for John to eat the scroll, and why is it important for you and me to take in God's Word?

7. Describe your feelings toward God's Word.

8. How are you personally contributing to getting the gospel to the world?

CHAPTER SIXTEEN

Who Will be Christ in Our Most Crucial Hour?

REVELATION 11

"Meanwhile, in a panic, healthy people did all they could to avoid the sick. Doctors refused to see patients; priests refused to administer last rites; and shopkeepers closed their stores. Many people fled the cities for the countryside, but even there they could not escape the disease."
–History.com *editors, June 2, 2019*

The year was 1347. October came as had many other Octobers, but this year would be different. In that month, 12 ships from the Black Sea docked at the Sicilian port of Messina. All of Europe was not ready for what was on board. On board were many who were already dead, but still others were carrying the bubonic plague. Over the next five years, Black Death would kill more than 20 million people in Europe – almost one-third of the continent's population. One would think the church would stand up, but the established church did just the opposite. First-hand accounts tell of the cowardness and faithlessness of the church in running away from their opportunity to show the world Christ in its most crucial hour.

In every generation there seem to be moments of crisis where the Lord offers the church an opportunity to be His ambassadors of mercy and hope. Paul writing to the church at Corinth outlined the above truth so well when he wrote:

> "God entrusted to us (the church) the message of reconciliation. Therefore, we are ambassadors for Christ; God making his appeal through us. We implore you on behalf of Christ, be reconciled to God" (II Cor. 5:19b-20).

As I write this chapter, the headlines in our world are filled with chaos, nations on the verge of war, and our own nation deeply divided. At the same time, some of the greatest preachers of our day have been called home to Jesus. I see churches that are fighting for internal control while the world is perishing without a witness. Even worse are those who claim to be God's ambassadors but have chosen a path of either hiding from the war or trying to simply exist in silence.

I cry out. Who will be Christ in our most crucial hour? This, brothers and sisters, is a day of urgency.   Could it be that the events predicted in the book of Revelation are upon us? If they are, and many of us believe they are about to begin if they are not already in the early stages, who will be God's final witnesses?

As we turn the page in our Bibles to Revelation eleven, we are about to be introduced to two special witnesses who God uses in miraculous ways. But before we consider their place in prophecy, let us consider two things:

JOHN WAS BEING ENCOURAGED TO COMPLETE HIS RECORDING OF THE EVENTS OF THE LAST DAYS.

In our last chapter we read about how John needed to be encouraged by God to complete his assignment. The truth is, we all need to be encouraged to complete our assignments from God. It was young Timothy who needed God's encouragement to complete his assignment as the pastor in the church at Ephesus (I Timothy 1:1-6). It was the prophet Elijah who wanted to run away and hide from his assignment (I Kings 19). God came to Elijah and spoke in a small still voice, reminding him that He (God) had work for him to do. Revelation ten and eleven are God's clear words of encouragement to John and to the church to complete our assignments.

JOHN WAS ASKED TO CARRY OUT A TASK THAT SEEMS INSIGNIFICANT, BUT IT WAS VERY SIGNIFICANT.

Here we see the Temple rebuilt, fulfilling prophecy (Ezek. 40-48; Zech. 6:12-13). At this point, three-and-one-half years of tribulation have been completed. The nation of Israel is turning back to the true and living God. MacArthur correctly helps us to understand this significant task given to John:

> "This is God reminding us that He has set aside Israel (the temple and altar) for His protection. God would deliver His people. Outside the temple was the Court of the Gentiles, who had been hearing the gospel for generations, but now they will fall to the Anti-

christ's tactics. There will still be Gentiles saved during the tribulation, but now the Antichrist will dominate this period of three-and-one half years." (MacArthur, 295-296).

The first three-and-one-half years of the tribulation will be easy for Israel, but now the Antichrist will no longer tolerate anyone worshipping the true and living God. These last three plus years before the Lord's return will be the most wicked and violent days of the world's history. Jesus spoke of these days, "And if those days had not been cut short, no human being would be saved. But for the sake of the elect those days will be cut short" (Matt. 24:22).

Question: Who will stand up for God in the midst of days of wickedness and violence? John writes, "and I will grant authority to my two witnesses…"

There will be two people (unknown by name) who will minister in the last three-and-one-half years of the Great Tribulation. They are only identified as "Two olive trees and two lampstands that stand before the Lord on the earth." Bible Scriptoriums will know this is a prophetic quote from Zechariah 4:1-14. We know olive oil was placed in lamps that were used to light the night for all who needed to see their way through the dark. Here we see two witnesses who were:

• Lights to a dark world

These two were carrying God's Word to light the way (Psalm 119:105) for a world that needed the truth. These men were shining the light of revival to a nation in the darkness. These two were being used by God. God also calls each of His witnesses to do the same today (Matt. 5:13-16).

Here we see two witnesses who also were:

- **Broken for their world**

They were, according to John, "clothed in sackcloth." We know this to be clothing worn in the Old Testament days by those who were grieving and mourning. The great prophet Daniel wore sackcloth as he mourned for his people (Dan. 9:3). In Romans 9:1-3, Paul was broken for his own people. Are there any witnesses today who are compelled to go as witnesses because of their brokenness?

Here we see two witnesses who were:

- **Powerful in their world**

This is all out war as these two witnesses stand for God. The enemy wanted to kill them, but God protected them (I John 5:18). The enemy hated their message. I understand the enemy's hatred as these witnesses predicted the woes that were coming. I imagine the world's anger growing as the Seal Judgments and now the Trumpet Judgments came. These were God's messengers of repentance, but the world was not repenting. The world had to be vicious in their desperate hate of these men. MacArthur writes:

> "These men will have power to shut up the sky. People's torment will be greatly intensified when the third trumpet judgement comes, resulting in the poisoning of one-third of the earth's fresh water supply (8:10-11). Throughout their entire preaching there will be a drought in the world. Devastation will be everywhere." (MacArthur, 302)

Brothers and sisters, we need to know God's Word. God's Word is our power through the Holy Spirit in our world. We are called to cry out, "Repent for the Kingdom of God is at hand." We are called to be powerful in calling men and women, boys and girls everywhere to be saved today (II Cor. 6:1-2).

John writes these two witnesses are invincible until their assignment is finished. I believe they finish just before the last bowl judgment. The Bible says, God allows the Antichrist to kill the two witnesses. We ask, "What is this Lord?" But wait, the Lord is not finished with these men.

Here we see two witnesses who were:

• **Resurrected before the world**

Here we see the world rejoicing because of the taking out of the two witnesses who they believed had caused all of the tribulation. They so hated these two that they would not even allow them to have a decent burial. The whole world has thrown a party believing the enemy is destroyed. But God is not through with these witnesses. Suddenly, as the world watches through media, God places resurrection life in these two witnesses.

Before a watching world, God says, "**Come up here.**"

Brothers and sisters, how can we not be encouraged to be a witness for the God who says, "even if we die, we will live again" (John 11:25-26). He is the God who is the resurrection and the life (John 10:17-18).

As the world watches in silence, heaven receives its witnesses home!!!

Please do not stare too long here; look back at what happens. One tenth of the city of Jerusalem is destroyed. Seven thousand people died, and the rest in the city turned to the Lord. God is keeping His promise to Israel (Rom. 11:4-5).

Before we can pause to ponder what we have just read, the Bible says, "The second woe is past and the third is coming quickly."

What do we take from this today? I believe there are **three truths and one challenge**:

1. The eternal God is coming to fulfill His plan to reclaim the earth (Vs: 17).

2. The eternal God is coming to judge those who stood against Him (Vs: 18a).

3. The eternal God is coming to reward those who lived and live for Him (Vs: 18b).

HERE IS OUR CHALLENGE:

God has called the church to engage in being His witness in these last days. We have two models called witnesses before us. Let us not be like other generations who hide in the day of adversity. Nor may we live in silence. Let's accept God's challenge to be a witness in our day -souls are depending on it!!!

STUDY QUESTIONS:

1. Why does it seem so difficult to share the gospel in our culture today? Give illustrations with your answer.

2. Who do you believe the two special witnesses are? Give reasons for your answers.

3. Define the word "witness" in Biblical terms.

4. What does the Bible mean by "Fire pours from their mouth and consumes the foes?"

5. Describe in your own words, "God's judgment on the dead."

6. What is the Ark of the Covenant and its significance in Revelation 12?

7. What does the Bible mean by the second "woe?" Give illustrations with your answers.

8. Is there really life after death? Give reasons for your answer.

CHAPTER SEVENTEEN

Making Sense Out of Life, Pt. 1

REVELATION 12

"Armageddon is upon us, what will we do? Get the details you need,"
–Hal Lindsey.

The year was 1999, the world was preoccuppied with Y2K. Many labeled the problem as the Y2K bug. The problem related to the formatting and storage of calendar data for dates beginning January 1, 2000. Many thought that at midnight all electrical devices would cease, and people everywhere were told to stock up on water and food. Many said, this will be the end. But as you can already tell, the world did not end, and we are still here.

I still remember those days leading up to January 1, 2000, and I still remember the uneasiness in my own life. Someone in our church bought us a generator for our safety. Many in our church, including Sherry and myself, stocked up on water and canned goods (which we used for the next year). I can still remember staying up that New Year's Eve night to see if anything happened. When it didn't, most of us felt silly, and many preachers who predicted the end, lost credibility.

The urgency people had in the last months of 1999 was replaced by apathy, and most churches went back to business as usual. Peter wrote about such people in II Peter 3:4 "They will say, where is the promise of His coming? For ever since the fathers fell asleep, all things are continuing as they were from the beginning of creation."

Could it be that the urgency we have been reading about is unfounded? Could it be that there is no need for urgency? As we come to chapter 12 in the book of Revelation, the Seventh Trumpet of God has sounded. The wrath of God is being released, and the true end of the world as we know it was before John.

Since the fall of humanity, the world has been moving toward this moment. The nations have raged, but the end is coming. Here before us in chapters 12-14, God pulls back the curtain from the judgment itself and reveals to us all that has been going on and is going on in the world.

I wrote the following in a sermon back in 2014:

> "There has been a battle raging since the beginning of time. It began with Satan who rebelled against God. His name was Lucifer (Is. 14:11-14). He was God's top angel. But he desired to take over heaven. He had secured the support of one-third of all the angels of heaven. He was cast out of heaven with his rebellious angelic team (Ezek. 28:12-17). Down to the earth he came after creation to tempt Adam and Eve to join his team. They did join his team in Genesis 3. At that moment in history, all of humanity was plunged into sin and rebellion. Since that day until this day, the battle between the forces of heaven and hell have continued to

rage." (Keith Joseph, Sermon *"Whose Side Are You On?* July 13, 2014)

In these chapters there are seven visions given to John. These visions help us to make sense out of this life which seems so filled with battles. In this chapter we are going to discover the opposing leaders of the battle. We will also discover what the opposing sides are doing in the battle of life. Finally, we will discover how to be on the winning side

WHO ARE THE OPPOSING LEADERS IN THE BATTLE?

In verses 1-2 we read about God's team and His Leader, our Messiah (Jesus Christ). Maybe you ask, how did you get this out of these verses? The answer comes from the Old Testament (Gen. 37:9; Isa. 54:6-7). These verses reveal Israel to be the woman, and Jesus to be the one inside of Israel's womb. According to Romans 9:4-5, it was Israel who gave us our Messiah.

In verses 3-5 we read about the opposing team and its leader. The leader is (the great red dragon) Satan himself, and his team is the one-third of the angels of heaven who rebelled with him. Adrian Rogers writes:

> "Satan had seven heads, ten horns, and seven crowns. Seven means perfection and ten means complete. Horns in the Bible are symbolic of power, so when you put seven and ten together, these things are symbolic of Satan's diabolical earthly power and wisdom." (Rogers, 144)

WHAT ARE THE OPPOSING SIDES
DOING AND WHAT ARE THEIR GOALS?

Israel is laboring in pain. She is tormented, tossed about, and harassed by the enemy who wants to keep the Messiah from coming. Here we see in verses 4-6 that Satan has been trying to stop Jesus from coming. For 4000 years he tried to stop Jesus from coming. He understood what God had said would happen. This is why over and over he tried to destroy Israel. We remember Exodus 2 when there was an attempt to genocide all the Jewish boys. Satan was behind it all. David was almost destroyed by Saul. MacArthur correctly observes: "During the days of the divided kingdom, the messianic line was twice dwindled to one fragile child," (MacArthur, IBID, Vol. 2, 10).

I have good news, Satan failed. Verse 5 overviews Jesus' incarnation, life, death, burial, resurrection and ascension. Hamilton writes:

"When Jesus died on the cross, it looked like Satan had conquered. But God turned certain and total defeat - his own people rejecting and crucifying the Messiah - into the victory that saves the world. When it looked like the last defense against evil had fallen, Christ rose from the dead, decisively breaking the back of evil." (Hamilton, 249).

Between verses 5 and 6 John brings us back to our place in time. The Bible says that the nation of Israel is protected by God (we are now at the mid-way point of the Tribulation). In this moment in time the war is about to heat up. The Ark Angel Michael announces to Satan, "you can no longer come up here." Until this point Satan has had access to heaven, not as a resident, but as an accuser of the brethren (12:10). But no more.

For the last half of the Tribulation, Satan's place will be totally on the earth. You and I need to take notice of this. When this happens things on the earth that are already wicked are about to be taken to a new level of wickedness. Pay close attention here; Satan knows his time is short! The death sentence and date have been handed down. Satan knew this was coming. His demons meeting with Jesus asked, "Have you come to torment us before the time?" (Matt. 8:29)

HOW CAN WE BE ON THE WINNING SIDE?

I cannot speak for your life, but I can speak for my life, "I do not want to be on the losing side." It is certain that some who read this have no clue of what you are reading. You have lived your life under the deception of Satan. He is the master deceiver, (John 8:44) and Satan has led you astray and kept you in the dark all of your life. Isn't it time to wake up and embrace the winning side?

John tells us how to get on the winning side:

1. You must surrender your life to the resurrected lamb of God (Jesus Christ).

Jesus was victorious over Satan at the cross. It is His blood that cleanses us (I John 1:7; Eph. 1:7). Adrian Rogers writes "You will never have victory over Satan as long as there is unconfessed, unrepentant sin in your life." (Rogers, 149). It is Jesus Christ's blood that frees us from the bondage of sin and the wrath of God. It is our testimony to our belief in Jesus which becomes our witness before Satan. He can no longer have reign in our lives (I John 5:18).

2. You must stay on the winning side by a faith witness in the resurrected lamb of God.

As Satan's anger heats up, you are not going to back down. God has given you the spirit of power, love, and a sound mind. Your victory has already been won. You are called to walk in the same blessing that God promised to the church at Philadelphia (3:1). God will keep you (protect) you in the hour of trial.

3. You must have courage as a member of the resurrected team.

Yes, you and I might be called to give our lives in the struggle. John wrote, "They kept on loving Jesus even in spite of coming death." These believers knew there was rest beyond the river of martyrdom. In chapter 13 we are called to endure as Children of God. In chapter 14 we are reminded of this truth: "Blessed indeed," says the Spirit, "that they may rest from their labors, for their deeds follow them."

At this moment the battle is raging, and the battle is revealing the opposing sides. At this moment the world is making its choice as to which side it will be on. It is now reality time for you and me, which team will we side with?

STUDY QUESTIONS:

1. What has been God's purpose for Israel since her beginning days?

2. Why did God decide for Jesus to be born in a Jewish family?

3. Why did the Jewish people reject Jesus?

4. Why does Satan hate Jesus and His church?

5. What signs of the end are you seeing in our day? Give illustrations in your answer.

6. What fears do you have in sharing your faith?

7. Who is Michael, and why did he deliver God's message to Satan?

8. What will you take away from this week's study?

CHAPTER EIGHTEEN

Making Sense Out of Life, Pt. 2

REVELATION 13:1-14:5

"If I am ever really in power, the destruction of the Jews
will be my first and most important job. As soon as I have
power, I shall have gallows after gallows erected, for example,
in Munich on the Marienplatz - as many of them as traffic allows."
–Adolph Hitler, 1922

How could anyone hate a people group so much that they would seek its total annihilation? One only has to look back in history to find an answer. As a child, Adolph Hitler had been mistreated by Jewish people, and he grew up with a hatred that consumed him. Hitler said he "would not rest until every city in Germany was cleansed of the last Jew!" (John Toland, *Adolph Hitler* [London: Book Club Associates, 1977], p.116).

As one studies church history it seems that God's people have always been under the eye of a world bent on her destruction. Even as I write this chapter, the climate in the country that I love seems to be leaning more and more to anti-Christian views. In some places in

America it is not safe for a Christian to go out alone at night. For some people there is an uneasiness about the future of Christianity in our nation. Hear me brothers and sisters, I do not find myself in a position of fear or uneasiness. I find myself in a position of great faith in being urgent about the day in which I live, because this could possibly be the generation that sees the Second Coming of the Lord.

We know the battle is certainly not new, and the battle is certainly not being fought with new weapons. The opposite is the case. David Jeremiah writes: "Satan has very few weapons in his arsenal, but he is very good with the weapons he possesses." (David Jeremiah, *Everything You Wanted to Know About Spiritual Warfare* [San Diego , Turning Point for God,2004], 45).

You and I must remember the battle has been going on since the fall of mankind. This battle, since its beginning, has been about control of the universe with humans being simply pawns in Satan's hand. Satan never cared, nor does he care, about humanity. Only God cared enough about humanity to send His Son to become the ransom for our victory in the battle.

Question: Are you locked in a battle in your life? Do you find yourself under constant bombardment with trials and tragedies on every corner? Recently I met a person who said, "Pastor, I just seem to go from one tragedy to the next." This person was evidencing a life-story of Satan's control over her.

In these middle chapters in the book of Revelation (12-14), John is helping us to make sense out of the battles that have been raging since the fall. In chapter twelve John gave us an overview of that battle. We saw God's choosing of a people and His giving that people a child (Jesus Christ), and we saw Satan attempting to destroy that child. We were reminded how the enemy could not defeat Jesus, so instead, he comes after God's people. The chapter ends with the sobering reality of Satan knowing his time was short.

Question: Are you on the Lord's team or are you on Satan's team? So many people have not decided in their minds as to which team they are on. Be assured, Jesus said in Luke 11:23, either you are on His team or you are against His team. I want to say, once a person makes sense of what is happening in the war, usually he or she changes sides. Usually they come to Jesus because His is the winning side. This is so important to know because there is coming a day when the last battle will be fought between heaven and hell.

Here in chapter thirteen, John teaches us about this future battle. One might ask, "How many more wars will the world have to endure before the end comes?" Only God knows the answer to this question. But there is one thing I know, when the last battle comes, I want to be on the Lord's side.

There are two important assignments I want to put before you in this chapter:

PAY ATTENTION TO SATAN
AND HIS LEAD TEAM

We remember from our last chapter that Satan's forces are the one-third of the angels who sided with him (Lucifer) when he rebelled against God (12:4). Now we are made aware that he recruits humans to be on his team. In particular he recruits (in the days of the Tribulation) two people to be on his lead team.

In Revelation 13 these people are identified as beast one and beast two. Be assured they have nothing in common with Thing 1 and Thing 2. We know these beasts as The Antichrist and The False Prophet.

Notice beast one rises out of the sea (speaking about the nations of the world). This man comes from the sea of humanity (Rev 17:15). He has great power to form coalitions with nations (signified by his ten horns and seven heads). Daniel 7:24 speaks about his power to control nations. Many believe he will revive the Roman Empire (referring to the beast being described as a leopard, bear, and lion).

One thing is for sure, Satan believes this man can lead the world to worship at his feet. This is why he gives all his power to his work (13:2b). This Antichrist works all kinds of miracles (counterfeit). He is the lawless one mentioned in II Thessalonians 2:9. His power seems to be so great that he is killed and raises himself from the dead. By the climax of the Tribulation period, he has the entire world (except God's chosen ones) worshipping at his feet.

One might ask, where is God in all of this? Has God lost his power? Does Satan now have the upper hand? The answer is no. John writes, "Satan was allowed to exercise authority…" This is all in the very plans of God. How do I know this to be? For one thing, in 580 B.C. Daniel prophesied about these coming events. The Lord knew because He is sovereign, and He set it all up so that humanity might reveal whose side she is on and so that Satan would go all-in against God. In doing so, the last battle would come.

In the last half of the Tribulation, the Antichrist will assume complete control of the world system. He will abolish all other religions except his own (II Thess. 2:4).

Here are two sobering realities in verses eight through ten:

1. All those who are not Christians will fall down and worship the Antichrist. Even those who say they are Christians and are not.

2. God's people will have to take their stand in the Great Tribulation. There will be no half-in or casual believing. There will no longer be any churches that are Six-Flags over Jesus. You will be either all-in with your life on the line or you will be on Satan's team led by the Antichrist.

But wait, there is another person on the lead team, we see him in (13:11-18). This beast is described as "rising out of the earth." The word earth means what it says, someone who lives on the earth. This second beast we know as the False Prophet whose entire purpose is to represent the Antichrist. He leads the entire world in the worship of the Antichrist. He leads in setting up an image of the Antichrist in the Temple. He even seems to have the power to give life to the image. This clearly fulfills II Thess. 2:4.

This false prophet seems to be a strong religious leader, but the truth is, he is more vile than Hitler ever thought about being. Now that the Antichrist is in control of the world, he is able to even control all commerce. The world will be forced to bow at his feet before they can buy, sell, or even eat. They must submit to a mark known by the church as 666 (The Mark of the Beast). All who refuse will do so at the cost of their lives. For three-and-one-half years there will be the day in and day out genocide of all who refuse to follow the Antichrist.

For all who read this, it is a good time to summarize what we have just read. John has revealed to us the false trinity. Satan wants to be in the place of God the Father. He has empowered the Antichrist to replace Jesus. He has raised up the False Prophet to take the place of the Holy Spirit.

I love what John Walvoord wrote:

"Probably the best interpretation is that the number six is one less than the perfect number seven, and the threefold repetition of the six would indicate that for all their pretentions to deity, Satan and the two beasts were just creatures and not the Creator." (John Walvoord, *The Bible Knowledge* Commentary [Wheaton Ill, Victor books, 1985], 983).

Oh, my friend, God is still in charge of all the events of this world. The battle is raging, but He is coming to end all battles. This leads me to the second assignment:

PLEASE DECIDE NOW TO
BE ON JESUS' TEAM

The first five verses of chapter fourteen mention a select group of people we have already met back in Revelation 7. (Please refer back to chapter 13 for a detailed study of their ministry in the Tribulation). Here we are told the Lord had brought them through the Tribulation.

These did not take the Mark of the Beast (13:17). We see by the description of their purity that they have been marked by the Cross of Christ (Gal. 6:14). These stood the test, they lied not about their faith. They were followers of Christ, and they were willing to put their lives on the line for the gospel of the Lord Jesus Christ.

These would become the first of many who triumphed through the power of the Lamb. The question comes to mind so clearly, why are you not on Jesus' team? How could you possibly side with one who wants to overthrow the God who created you? Satan wants to overthrow the God who cares for you. He wants to overthrow God, and if you are destroyed in the crossfire, he could not care less. And finally, who wants to go to hell with Satan? By the way, this is where he is headed, along with the False Prophet and the Antichrist (19:20; 20:10).

I plead with you to decide this day to be on Jesus' team. For those who are already on Jesus' team, I plead with you to grow in your understanding of how to share your faith and to know your faith. If you are alive in the Great Tribulation, you will be counted on to witness for Him.

This week's questions will stir our hearts to both see where we are and what we need to do to be on the winning team.

STUDY QUESTIONS:

1. Who is the Antichrist, and could he be alive today?

2. What is the difference between the Antichrist in Revelation 13 and the one mentioned by John in I John 2:19?

3. Write out how a person gets on God's team.

4. Describe the job of the False Prophet in the Great Tribulation.

5. How will we be able to recognize a believer in the Tribulation period?

6. How difficult will it be to follow Christ in the Great Tribulation?

7. If it is more difficult in the Great Tribulation to follow Jesus, then why do we seem to make it so difficult today?

8. When will the end come? Check out I Thessalonians 5:1-5 before you give your answer.

CHAPTER NINETEEN

Making Sense Out of Life, Pt. 3
REVELATION 14:6-20

"Hear this, you elders; give ear, all inhabitants
of the land! Has such a thing happened in
your days, or in the days of your fathers?" –Joel 1:2

I had to be no more than seven years old when my grandfather sat down with me to have "the talk." Now before you think that I am going to get too personal, I am not referring to the talk about the birds and bees. No, my grandfather was going to have "the talk" with me. The talk which literally caused me to have nightmares for weeks after. What was the talk? The talk was about the coming of the end of the world.

My grandfather was an avid reader of the Bible, and he was an avid reader of a magazine entitled "The Plain Truth" published by Garner Ted Armstrong. My grandfather presented to me a very convincing case as to when the world was coming to an end. He even had charts that he had gotten from "The Plain Truth." My grandfather shared explicit details about how Christians would have their heads cut off if they rejected the Mark of the Beast, and he shared how no Christians would be cast in Hell when the Lord returned. By the time he was finished with "the talk," I knew Jesus was coming back in 1974. But as you obviously know, Jesus did not come back in 1974.

However, Jesus is coming back again. I take you back to one of our first chapters of study when John recorded the following words, "Behold, He is coming with the clouds, and every eye will see Him, even those who pierced Him, and all the tribes of the earth will wail on account of Him…" (1:7).

John predicts a day when all will see Him. The question I have for you in this chapter is simple, are you starting to make sense of what is happening in our day? I truly believe we can look back through 6000 plus years of history and see the battle between God and Satan. I think it will be clear to those who believe the Bible when the Antichrist steps onto the scene of history. But what will not be clear is the exact time when it will happen.

You see, someone can figure out the battle but still fail to make the correct decision. In Revelation 14 we find John's final overview about the Great Tribulation. By the way, chapter 14 ends at the scene of the last great battle which is identified in chapter 16 as the Battle of Armageddon (16:16).

There are three scenes before us in this chapter:

THE SCENE OF THE ONE
FINAL CALL OF THE GOSPEL

John records an angel coming from Heaven preaching the eternal gospel for one last time. Surely by now the world would have turned, but still they have not believed the gospel. The gospel is the good news about the bad news. The good news is, God has a remedy for our sin.

That remedy is Jesus (John 3:16; Col. 1:13-14; Eph. 1:7, 2:13-16). But the gospel is also the bad news about the good news. If a person rejects Jesus as Lord and Savior, he or she has no hope of eternal life in Heaven. How and why would God the Father allow someone into His Heaven who hates His Son and lives as a rebel against God's Kingdom? In verse seven we are taught to have great love and awe for our Holy God. A lost world will be without excuse when they stand before God.

THE SCENE OF THE ONE-WORLD GOVERNMENT AND RELIGION FALLING

The second angel proclaims the good news of Babylon's falling. Despite all of Satan's efforts to overthrow the throne of Heaven with his dream team of the Antichrist and the False Prophet, his kingdom falls. The very system the world bought into has come up short. In chapter 16 we will see God's wrath being poured out against this wicked one-world government.

THE SCENE OF ONE OPTION FOR THOSE WHO HAVE REJECTED JESUS

In verses nine through eleven we discover the angel's announcement that all who have followed Satan will receive the same judgment as Satan. Hell will be the eternal residence of all who reject Jesus. This is a lost person's one option at death. Please do not believe you will just be hanging out with all your friends in hell.

Surely you do not think that this judgment is simply a slight slap on the hand that will go away shortly. Surely you do not believe this is a go to jail card in Monopoly where you can get out of jail after three rolls of the dice. Surely you understand the words "full strength."

God's wrath will not be diluted because you have a grandmother who loves Jesus. For eternity all who reject Jesus will have no rest day or night in the pain called judgment. Every hour of every day rebels will exist seeing the angels and Jesus in Heaven.

Rebellion is put down in hell, but the rebel's heart will still be intact, this is why judgment continues day and night forever and ever. Someone commented to Adrian Rogers, "Preacher, isn't all this stuff just symbolic?" Here was Dr. Rogers' response: "For your sake, I hope it is not symbolic if you die and go to hell; the symbolism is always weaker than the reality." (Rogers, 178).

Question: Are you moving beyond making sense to the place where you realize you need to make a decision to change teams, or maybe you have family members you know who need to change teams?

As God's child, I do not fear the coming judgment of God, because He is my Lord and Savior. I endure what is happening in our world (14:12) knowing there is a better day coming. I rejoice, because I know there is a day when I will lay my burdens down (14:12). But what about those who reject Jesus, or those who say, I will follow Him some day, but then wait until it is too late.

Look in your Bibles at chapter 14 and verse 14 where we see one bonus scene.

THE SCENE OF THE ONE BATTLE
WHERE NO LOST PERSON SURVIVES

In these verses there is the judgment of God being compared to a farmer with his sickle reaping the harvest of both over ripe and fully ripe grapes. The imagery could not be clearer. This is the Son of God (Jesus) coming in wrath to judge the world.

John MacArthur is correct when he writes:

"Armageddon will actually be a slaughter rather than a battle. When the Lord Jesus returns, the Antichrist, the False Prophet, and all their human and demonic forces will be immediately destroyed, Rev. 19:11-21." (MacArthur, Vol 2, 116).

John describes the scene as the most horrible blood bath of the ages. He describes the blood from the slaughter covering 184 miles with its height reaching that of a horse's bridle. I personally have stood in the very valley where most believe this battle will take place. This valley is one of the most fertile and beautiful spots on the planet.

As I stood there years ago, I thought, this is the path sin takes in a world bent on following Satan. So now you have it, Revelation 12, 13, and 14. Have you made sense out of it all? I understand if it is hard because I have been studying this book for almost thirty years and I still scratch my head at times. However, even when I can't comprehend it all, I believe.

Yes, since 1974 when my grandfather had "the talk," it set me on a path that would lead me, in that same year, to put all my faith in Jesus Christ as my Lord and Savior. I truly believe God used my grandfather's passion for letting me know the truth to lead me to follow Jesus as Lord and Savior.

It is my prayer that you allow this book called "Revelation" to lead to your genuine faith in Jesus Christ. I also pray that you would allow this book to create an urgency in your heart to reach people with the everlasting gospel while there is still time.

STUDY QUESTIONS:

1. How many times have you personally heard the gospel? Describe the day you accepted the gospel, if you have.

2. Describe in your own words, the pros and cons of a one-world government? Consider Jesus coming to rule in a one-world government as part of your answer.

3. What does John mean by "drinking the wine of the passion of her sexual immorality?"

4. Explain the significance of John describing the pain of hell as being "fire and sulfur?"

5. Why will Christians be able to rest from their labors when they die? Explain what this means to you personally.

6. What happens when Jesus reaps the earth in Vs: 16?

7. Do you really believe there will be blood running to the horse's bridle for 184 miles? Explain why you do or why you do not believe?

8. In what ways has this chapter challenged you? Share your answers with the group.

CHAPTER TWENTY

The Last Round, Getting What We Deserve
REVELATION 15-16

*"For the wrath of God is revealed from heaven against
all ungodliness and unrighteous of men, who by their unrighteousness
suppress the truth." –(Romans 1:18)*

Question: Are there any innocent people in the world? This question was proposed by David Platt in his now bestselling book entitled, *Radical.* I still have etched in my mind his commentary. David wrote, "The premise of the question is flawed, because according to Scripture, there are no innocent people." Romans 3:23 settles the question for me.

The angel reminds us in chapter fifteen: "God is just and true in all of His ways."

Here in chapter fifteen we read of seven bowls. These bowls contain the last round of judgments coming from heaven. Keep in mind that these judgments are coming against those who are lined up with the Antichrist. The people of the world have become his prostitutes (This will make more sense after you read the next chapter). The people of world are rebels who are ripe for judgment.

In a few paragraphs I will begin to describe the seven last judgments. But before I do, I want to ask what you are doing with what you are learning in this study. You and I have been given the everlasting gospel, and we have been tasked to carry it to the nations. This is exactly what I am doing.

As I write this chapter on my iPad, I am currently at thirty-one-thousand feet in the air somewhere over the Gulf of Mexico. There are sixteen people on our team. We are headed to a remote island off the coast of Honduras. My prayer for this trip is simple: "May this island called Utila have ample cause to praise God because of our coming in the name of Christ."

We are headed to a place that knows not the gospel. There is not one person on the island who is innocent before God. But there is also not one person on the island that God does not love, and there is not one person on the island that God does not want to save (II Peter 3:9). But the following is also true, there is not one person who will be judged wrongly by God.

Can anyone, anywhere in the world, say that the last round of judgments is anything more than just judgment coming from almighty God? This world has rejected God's leadership for over six-thousand years. The angel correctly comments in chapter sixteen, "The world is getting what it deserves." Brothers and sisters, God is righteous in all of His actions with humanity (15:3-4).

I have come to believe if a person does not come to repentance before the Great Tribulation, he or she will not do so during the Great Tribulation. The apostle Paul writes about such people; "They will perish because they refused to love the truth and be saved" (II Thess. 2:10). When the Antichrist comes, such people will believe what is false (II Thess. 2:11-12). The Bible is clear, "such people have pleasure in unrighteousness." This is why chapter 16 must be read not as an innocent world suddenly facing attack by a heartless God, but as a world in open rebellion against God. I am telling you; You and I have only this very moment to decide. No one is promised tomorrow. (II Cor. 6:1-2).

This is why, with urgency, I am on this plane, and this is why our church travels wherever there is an open door. We go proclaiming the everlasting gospel. This is why last week I was at a youth camp, and this is why I am on this plane today. This is why Pastor Cary Snelling is leading a team to Romania next week. We are crying out everywhere, "Come to Jesus while there is time, for there may not be any time - after this time." Take this to heart, there will be a moment in time when the hour of judgment will come (14:7).

I can truly say I do not want anyone to perish because they have not heard. If you have any family members or friends who are not ready for the Lord's return, go to them now. Put this devotion book down and call them now. If not now, when? Be assured the Great Tribulation will not change their hearts! Only the everlasting gospel can change their hearts.

Now it is time to look deeply at the descriptions of the just judgments in chapter 16:

BOWL JUDGMENT ONE:
UNRELENTING PHYSICAL PAIN

God had promised (14:11) that there would be unrelenting torment and now it is here. The Bible clearly points out the people who are judged. They are those who "bore" the mark of the beast. They willingly and openly wore with pride the mark of who they worshipped. Their judgment from God was and is just.

I believe people, with the world's goods in their hands, will blame God for their just judgment. I believe people with the lust of sin in their hearts will accuse God of being unfair. Their judgment is just.

BOWL JUDGMENT TWO:
THE SEA WILL TURN TO BLOOD.

Imagine the horror and stench of everything living in the sea dying. The world will be dying in its own filth.

BOWL JUDGMENT THREE:
THE DRINKING WATER IS NOW GONE.

Life cannot exist much longer. Doctors must admit humanity's days are numbered.

In this moment the angel brings up an important point. Humanity has brought this judgment upon itself. God has considered the matter for six-thousand years. He sent Jesus to be our remedy, and those who have taken the remedy are no longer under judgment. The angel proclaims: "They deserve this." Literally they are worthy of this. Brothers and sisters, this prefigures the final judgment in Rev. 20:13. "Humanity is judged according to their works." Now, we do not have to debate the issue. All men have crossed the deadline with God. Do you hear the words around the altar? "God, you are just."

Before we can linger here any longer, the next angel comes.

BOWL JUDGMENT FOUR:
THERE IS A CONSUMING SUN.

If you have ever been to the beach and laid out in the sun too long you know what this is like, except it will be a hundred times worse.

Man is scourged with the heat. This, brothers and sisters, must be just a taste of what hell will be like. As I write, I wonder who around me on this plane is not ready to meet the Lord.

Here, we are reminded in these verses of the very depths of humanity's rebellion, even a consuming sun does not turn the hearts of the people toward repentance. It is true, the Antichrist has convinced the world to drink dry the delusion of his perversion.

BOWL JUDGMENT FIVE:
DARKNESS OVER THE LAND

We praise our God that the kingdom of the Antichrist (16:10) is now plunged into darkness. This kingdom is destroyed (Rev. 17-18). But notice, the world mourned the loss of its source of pleasure and praise. The Bible says, "They cursed God." This means they slandered Him. All who trusted in the Antichrist are in shock, dealing with anger, and they are looking for someone to blame. It is God they blame.

BOWL JUDGMENT SIX:
THE BATTLE OF ARMAGEDDON

God dries up the great river Euphrates which has kept the nations of the world from converging on Israel for one last war. Hamilton comments: "The demons (even now) are hard at work constructing the plausibility structure that will convince people to go to war against the almighty" (Hamilton, 319).

BOWL JUDGMENT SEVEN:
IT IS DONE.

The announcement is made, "Judgment is completed." God has poured out all of His wrath. Now the world sees the devastation, and it is all but over. The beloved capital of the empire of the Antichrist is broken into three pieces. Surely the world will bow in honor to God now. We will have to wait until chapter 19 to see the answer.

However, I think you already know the answer. The world sees no wrong in their actions. If the judgments began today, would men repent? Today is still the age of grace, and today is all we have. When judgment begins, men's hearts will be steeped in rebellion against God.

As I finished the last sentence, I paused and looked to my right. Outside my window is an amazing scene of blue with the formation of the most amazing clouds. Great and amazing are the deeds of Holy God. I cannot imagine the change that is coming to this earth when judgment comes.

Brothers and sisters, this leads me to cry out, Lord help the church to reach this generation before the end. Oh my, the pilot has just announced that we are about to land. Where has the time gone? It's time for me to do what I came here to do!!! I pray you will do what you are called to do because the days are flying by.

STUDY QUESTIONS:

1. Describe in your own words the righteous acts of God.

2. Do you agree or disagree? The world will get what she deserves.

3. Will people who reject the gospel before the Great Tribulation have an opportunity to be saved during? Give reasons for your answer.

4. Why would people in the Great Tribulation refuse to follow Jesus?

5. Explain the significance of the unclean spirits looking like frogs.

6. Why will God bless the ones who stay awake (I Thess. 5:4-9)?

7. Explain "drinking the cup of God's wrath."

8. What does Scripture mean by "every island fled away and every mountain was no longer to be found."

9. What did God speak to you personally about in this study?

CHAPTER TWENTY-ONE

Whose Side are You On?

REVELATION 17:1-19:5

*"How horrible, fantastic, incredible it is that we
should be digging trenches and trying on gas masks here because
of a quarrel in a faraway country between people of whom we
know nothing." –Prime Minister Neville Chamberlain*

It was September 1938. Hitler was in the process of seizing Czechoslovakia. This country pleaded with Great Britain for help. But it fell on deaf ears because Prime Minster Chamberlain saw no need to get involved with what he thought was a small and isolated war. Little did he realize what was coming.

I believe people often read the book of Revelation with little urgency, because they believe the events could not even remotely happen in their day. It is true it has not happened in the two-thousand-plus years since God gave us this revelation. But consider this. For the first time in history, the events of the book of Revelation all seem to be feasible in our day.

As I write this, our nation and the nations of the world are facing new territory in their internal divisions, and the number of nations that have hate groups within them is at an all-time high. Could it be possible that the Antichrist is preparing to come even now? I am not trying to scare you. I am trying to help you awaken to the urgency of our day. I am afraid that most people fail to consider the signs around us. We are like the Prime Minister who believed what was happening would never affect him. But it did, and when the Great Tribulation comes, all the world will choose sides.

Let me take you back into the book of Revelation. As we left off last in our studies, the last Bowl Judgment had been unleashed on the world (16:17). The city of Babylon (16:18-19), the headquarters for the one-world government of the Antichrist, had been split into three parts. The world was left in a devasted place. The next event in chronological order will be "The Second Coming." But we will have to wait until chapter 19 to see this event.

As chapter 17 begins, we see a break, once again, in the narrative. Before us are two chapters of Scripture inserted by the Lord. "These two chapters go back to describe the world system led by Satan, the Antichrist, and the False Prophet, before God's judgment." (MacArthur, Vol 2, 157). The revelation here serves as God's next to the last call for humanity to wake up, come out, and follow Jesus.

The truth of these chapters cries out, "Whose side are you on?" The urgency of these chapters shakes me personally to the depths of my being. After seeing the truth about Satan and his world system, how could anyone buy into his world system, and how could anyone throw away their soul for the momentary pleasure of sin?

The angel reminds us the world is now under the spell of the Antichrist, "the dwellers on the earth have become drunk" (17:2). Here are three truths you need to understand before these chapters will make sense:

1. The *prostitute* symbolizes the one-world religion implemented by the Antichrist through the help of the False Prophet. Adrian Rogers reminds us, "Women in Bible prophecy are always considered a symbol of religion, whether good or bad" (Rogers, 192).

2. The *beast* is the Antichrist who controls the one-world government and who desires the worship of all people.

3. *Babylon* is the city where this one-world government and one-world religion has their headquarters.

In the first six verses of chapter 17, John describes the world's courtship with the prostitute. People from every nation, tribe, and tongue give their worship to the one-world system. Here before us are people and nations who are morally out of control and are seeking pleasure as their number one priority. This one-world system has given them everything they have ever wished for. They can have peace (thinking they are safe spiritually), and they can have pleasure (all the world's goods are for the taking). The world has totally disregarded the true and living God. Hamilton offers a revealing observation:

> "Rather than be faithful to God and render to Him what is due Him alone, the world's rulers have gone to the great prostitute by pursuing their own glory, their own name, their own purposes, all the while ignoring God's law" (Hamilton, 324).

While all religions are willingly bowing at the feet of the prostitute, there is one group who will not. We know these to be the saints of God. These are those whom the beast will martyr by the thousands (17:6). All of this horrifies John.

John cannot understand it all, but beginning in verse seven the angel explains the mystery. It is the Antichrist who has been behind this one-world religion (Prostitute). He has put together a coalition of leaders. All those who dwell on the earth who are not Christ-followers follow the Antichrist who faked his death and seems to have risen from the dead (13:3). For three-and-one-half-years (a little while) he has ruled. But this will not be enough for the Antichrist who is the puppet of Satan. He will come to do battle with Jesus (The Lamb).

But his battle is a useless battle. The last battle Jesus had was on the cross, and Satan lost there. But this time there is no cross; there is Jesus with the crown. He is Lord of Lords and King of Kings! He is coming to do battle, and with Him comes the church (17:18).

Notice there is one last footnote (17:15-19). The Antichrist, before this battle with the Lamb, turns on the prostitute. He cannot stand for anyone to share in the glory he desires. The leaders of the nations will join with the Antichrist, being directed by God, who has placed all of this in place, because the day of judgment has arrived.

It is at this point where I must ask again, whose side are you on?

Take time and consider your answer. You only have two options: God or Satan. "The one option serves the Lamb, the other the beast. The one-way lives for what will last forever, the other for what will look good for a short while before it is destroyed" (Hamilton, 323)

As chapter 18 opens, another angel comes with the news - the headquarters for the world system has fallen. Now the laughter of a rebellious world is coming to an end. There will be no more days of pleasure in sin.

Here are three imperatives that come from this chapter:

WAKE UP TO WHAT YOU
ARE A PART OF.

Chuck Swindoll puts this in terms we can understand.

"What if the entire world as you know it-people, things, events, and activities was suddenly to collapse? What if your sources of comfort, luxury, and entertainment were lost forever? Nobody wants the stock market to crash, the power grid to fail, or our cities to be leveled. The world wants the world to go on as it is" (Swindoll, 209).

But the world will not go on as it is, because the world is in self-destruct mode drinking the wine of perversion and loyalty to the wrong god. Friend, it is time to wake up to what you may be a part of.

COME OUT OF WHAT YOU
ARE A PART OF.

Verses four and five of chapter 18 offer this clear imperative. The words "come out," speak of ceasing to participate in the world system. As I read these words from Jesus again, I sense the kindness of God in giving people all this time to wake up and come out.

But I also sense the final warning of God to come out. If people do not come out, they will share in the same judgment as those who totally bought into the worship of the prostitute. God is not mocked, "for whatever a man sows he will also reap" (Gal. 6:7). Hell does not have to be your destiny; you can come out of your final approach to your final destination.

SURRENDER YOUR LIFE TO JESUS.

Look at all the devastation in chapter 18. The world mourns at the loss of the system that fueled their perversion. In one single hour the system was gone. Question, whose side are you on?

To be transparent with you, I am exhausted at this point in my writing. I have tried so hard to listen to the Holy Spirit and correctly interpret the text. I know the Lord is saying to some who read this, "wake up, come out, and surrender your life to me" (Jesus).

Hear the truth coming from the throne of God: "Salvation and glory and power belong to our God" (19:1). If you are on Satan's team, know that God stands at the door of your heart, ready to conquer Satan if you will surrender your life to Jesus (Rev. 3:20-21). Do it right now. If you are on God's team, take heart! You are on the conquering team. Being on the right team has eternal implications.

STUDY QUESTIONS:

1. Is it possible for the world to unite into one government and one religion? Give reasons for your answer.

2. What is the drawing card for the Prostitute?

3. What does the writer mean by "the earth's abominations?" (18:5)

4. Why will the Antichrist turn on the Prostitute?

5. What will happen when the one-world government collapses?

6. In 19:14 the Bible says, "The fruit for which your soul longed has gone from you." What fruit does your soul long for?

7. Why does God tell us to praise Him in 19:5? Is there any reason to praise God for the end of the Tribulation?

8. What did you take away from this week's study?

CHAPTER TWENTY-TWO

The Day We Live For

REVELATION 19:6-10

"My Lord. He calls me. He calls me by the thunder.
The trumpet sounds within my soul. I ain't got long to stay here.
Steal away. Steal away. Steal away to Jesus."

"As Charles Spurgeon's closest friends gathered around this very worn out pastor, he pushed himself up from the couch and joined in the circle of friends. A sting of pain rushed through Charles' swollen knees, but there was the sweetness of truth as Charles held other's hands with his swollen hands. He thought of Heaven, and he thought of Jesus. He joined in with the others with what faint voice he had, and he sang the above chorus." Cited from Pg. 219, *Steal Away Home*

It is a sad reality, but a reality we must all keep firmly before us: At some point the curse (Genesis 3) placed upon us will complete its full work, and we will die. Now there are many who meet with death from old age and many others from disease or tragedy. Whenever and however it comes, we want to be ready. But we also (as Christ-followers) want to live focused lives knowing there is a day we are each urgently looking forward to.

The day I am referring to is "the day we meet the Lord." Paul wrote about it in Philippians 3:20

"Our citizenship is in heaven from which also we eagerly wait for a Savior, the Lord Jesus Christ, who will transform the body of our humble state into conformity with the body of His glory."

There is coming a day when the church of the Lord Jesus Christ will be called home to be with Jesus. Whether this is at the rapture, as taught by many pastors in our day in reference to

(I Thess. 4:13-18; Rev. 4:2; John 14:2-3; I Cor. 15:50-58 and Matt. 24:44), or at the Second Coming as taught in Revelation 19, one thing is for sure, this is the day all who are in the church live for.

Can we truly say, we are ready to leave this world and move into the world to come? Paul spoke about "all who love His appearing," in II Timothy 4:8.

As we come to this section of Revelation, all of heaven is rejoicing because what the Apostles taught us and what the church longed for is finally taking place. Keep in mind where we are in the timeline of our study. The world has gathered (its armies) at the battle of Armageddon. The evil empire of the Antichrist has been destroyed, and the battle is about to take place. God is showing us those on the losing side (Rev. 17-18) and those on the winning side (Rev. 19:1-10).

If the church has been raptured out, then the saints of God (New Testament saints) will face the Judgment Seat of Christ (II Cor. 5:9-10) where our deeds will be evaluated and what was for ourselves will be deemed as worthless (I Cor. 3:11-16) and cast aside. But those deeds we did for the true glory of God will be rewarded by God. But if not, it is here in Revelation 19, when the Lord returns that the church will be raptured out at Jesus' Second-Coming. Either way, the church is delivered from the wrath of God. Both those who are Dispensational Premillennialist and those who are Historical Premillennialist believe the event before us is still to come. John identifies this event as "The Marriage Supper of the Lamb."

Notice in your Bible the text beginning in verse six: All those gathered in heaven are rejoicing because The Lord of heaven is coming down to reign. Write it down; Jesus is coming again. He is coming to rule and reign (Rev. 11:15, 17). All those gathered in heaven are rejoicing and giving honor and praise to the very one they have longed (all their lives on the earth) to meet.

Now the symbolism here needs explanation: God compares His (Jesus) relationship with the church as that of marriage. Scripture teaches us that Christ is the Bridegroom (John 3:27-30; Matt. 19: 15; 22:14). "Never has there been a more worthy bridegroom. Never has a man sacrificed more for his beloved. Never has a man gone to greater lengths, humbled himself more, endured more, or accomplished more in the great task of winning his bride." (Hamilton, 351).

Scripture also teaches us that the church is the Bride of Christ (Eph. 5:25-27). Chuck Swindoll gives us insightful help:

> "There are three parts to a Jewish wedding. There is the betrothal (Arranged by the parents). There is the journey of going to get the bride (Matt. 25:1-13). Finally, there is the ceremony when the marriage is consummated." This is for the church when all that we have entered into will now come to be (Swindoll, 242).

Let's attempt to put this together: On the day you received Jesus Christ as Lord and Savior you came to be in God's family. You were betrothed to Jesus. Paul writes about leading people in the city of Corinth to Jesus: "For I am jealous over you with godly jealousy: for I have espoused you to one husband, that I may present you as a chaste virgin to Christ" (II Cor. 11:2). In this moment, you are in the family, and in God's eyes you are His child (Rom. 8:14-18). But there is could be a long time between the day of God bringing you into the family and the day when you stand before Him consummated.

Back in Rev. 7:14 believers are clothed in white robes "washed and made white in the blood of Christ." We are positionally forgiven, but in the practice of our daily lives, people still know about our past, and they still see us when we do unrighteous deeds. But there is coming a day when we will no longer do unrighteous deeds, and there will be no more remembrance of our deeds (throughout eternity). We see this in (19:7), "The bride is ready."

Three truths should dominate our thoughts as we live for this day:

GOD IS CHANGING US
AS WE ANTICIPATE THAT DAY.

We are now in a new relationship, and God has made us new (II Cor. 5:17). We begin at salvation to do righteous deeds. "Greed turns to generosity because the Bridegroom has met our deepest need and will supply all our wants from His glorious riches. Lust gives way to contented joy in what we have, because the Bridegroom offers pleasures fuller and freer than anything the world has to offer" (Hamilton, 353).

We now live this life in anticipation of the life we have in the future. We are now citizens of another place, married to a Bridegroom who leads us in paths of righteousness for His name sake (Psalm 23:2).

GOD IS CALLING PEOPLE
TO BECOME PART OF HIS FAMILY.

John records the announcement of the angel: "Blessed are those who are invited to the marriage supper." It is true the Bridegroom and the Bride do not need to be invited because they are already a part of the wedding feast. Jesus met with a Centurion in Matthew 8. During the encounter about true faith, he made this proclamation,

> "And I say unto you, that many shall come from the east and west, and shall sit down with Abraham, and Isaac, and Jacob, in the kingdom of heaven" (Matt. 8:11).

John MacArthur comments:

> These people are not the church, they're a part of re-deemed Israel. There will be many others who are Jews, truly saved, proselytes to Judaism. Luke 13:28 says, "When you see Abraham and Isaac and Jacob and all the prophets in the Kingdom of God." I believe Old Testament saints are going to be a part of that, all the prophets, all the faithful, all the priests, all the believers redeemed by grace through faith, Enoch and Noah, all of them are going to be raised, according to Daniel Chapter 3. They're going to be raised, I believe, at the coming of Jesus Christ to set up His Kingdom. All of the hero's of Hebrews 11, they're all going to be there in the Kingdom. They're going to be the invited guests.

The Marriage Supper of the Lamb will be that moment in time when the Saints of all ages will be before the Lord in praise. Oh, what a day that will be! However, if the Lord returned now, how many in your family would not be there? This event leads me to get to work inviting others to come to Jesus. Luke 14:23 states "Go out and invite them to come in that my house will be filled."

JESUS IS THE CENTRAL FIGURE
AT THE MARRIAGE SUPPER OF THE LAMB.

Adrian Rogers: "The wedding does not center around the bride, but on the groom." (Rogers, 211). John is so taken with what he sees, that he falls to his knees and worships the angel. He is told, "Worship God."

This is where there is a great disconnect today. We find churches and Christians worshipping other things and other gods. Do we find the church in love with Jesus or do we find the church faltering in her love for Jesus? I think the answer lies in where a person is with Jesus.

In the hot sun of Malawi, the true Christians look forward to the Marriage Supper because all their poverty will be over. But in the American Church we sometimes wonder, what do we have to look forward to? Don't we have it all now? But wait, when trials come, when disease comes, when we become sick of all the world's goods which have not satisfied us, then we turn our attention toward another place and another person. Often God has to shake us up to get us to realize how important our marriage is to Him.

As I write this, I think of the words of the chorus again: "The trumpet sounds within my soul. I ain't got long to stay here. Steal away home." May that day make you live differently this day, with urgency for our Lord.

STUDY QUESTIONS:

1. What new insights have you gained from our studies this week?

2. Explain why so many Christians do not look forward to the return of the Lord.

3. Examine your life; what works of righteousness do you see in your life? Record your answers. What works of unrighteousness do you see in your life? Also record your answers.

4. How does the Marriage Supper encourage someone who is going through cancer?

5. What has Jesus (The Bridegroom) done so that you could be in God's family? List your answers and discuss in your Community Group.

6. Who will be at the Marriage Supper of the Lamb?

7. Why does the church seldom teach this section of Scripture? When was the last time you considered this event?

8. What will you do with your life now that you have read this chapter?

CHAPTER TWENTY-THREE

A Different Leader and a Different World

REVELATION 19:11-20:10

"You must come to my assistance, so that I may dispatch
the entire German Army as a birthday present to your Prince of Peace.
In exchange for four days of fighting weather, I will deliver You enough
Krauts to keep Your book-keepers months behind in the work. Amen."
—George Patton on the eve of the Battle of the Bulge.

On the eve of the Battle of the Bulge, it seemed as if it would be impossible for the American Third army, under the leadership of General George Patton, to deliver the trapped soldiers in Bastogne. The weather report was not favorable for a battle the next day. But on this night George Patton asked for the help of Almighty God. His words speak volumes to the carnage of war: "I am sick of this unnecessary butchering of American youth…" (O'Reilly, [New York, Henry Holt and Company] ,2014 131).

As I consider the state of our nation (The United Stated of America), the spiritual weather report is not favorable for life and peace. In recent days there have been two more shooting sprees in public places killing over thirty Americans. Instead of the nation coming together to fight against our common enemy who is Satan, we are divided over the issue of gun control. The issue is not gun control, the issue is simple; we are a nation that has lost her moral compass.

I ask myself, "What is the church to do?" I cry out to God, "Take charge of our land." With urgency I plead with God the Father to send us a different leader who will create a different world.

Brothers and sisters, the answer to my prayer is coming! The answer is in a person who is coming from heaven (19:11). He is the one John sees riding on a white horse which is the symbol of a conquering king who is taking leadership over the land that is to be his. The prophecies that follow give us joy in knowing there is going to be a new leader, and there is going to be a new world.

Let's examine what John writes under three headings:

WE SEE A NEW LEADER

If you have read the previous chapters in our study, you are familiar with who John is writing about in 19:11-12. The description John gives of this new leader is that he is none other than Jesus. These verses 11-16 present no less than three truths about this leader:

1. Jesus' character is unmatched by any leader in history (19:11-13).

This is why Jesus is on the White horse, not any other world leader from our history. Jesus alone is faithful (there is no record in history of even one unfaithful deed). Jesus alone is true. Every other leader has at least once told a lie, but never Jesus. Not only did He never lie, but He is truth itself. He is coming to make war on the unrighteousness of our world. He is coming to right every wrong. He will establish His throne as a place of righteous judgment. Look at the crowns on His head. He has all authority. No one else will be on the throne. We see His robe dipped in blood as one who does battle with the forces of the enemy.

Pay close attention (Vs: 13). He is called by his army, "The Word of God." "He is the full expression of the mind, will, and purpose of God, the radiance of His glory and the exact representation of His nature." (MacArthur, 218). It will be from His mouth that words of death will come to His enemies (19:15). This day He gives forth words of life to all who believe.

2. Jesus' power is unmatched by any army in history (19:14-21).

As John sees this vision of the new leader, the armies of the world have gathered against God Himself. We know this to be the Battle of Armageddon (16:16). All the great leaders with all of their man-made weapons will gather on this day. Never in history has such a day come. Never has so much destructive power been present in one place - at one time.

Look at the army of God (19:14). Who is this army, and what can they do? This army is made up of the following groups: God's glorified saints called the church, Tribulation believers, Old Testament Saints, and the Holy Angels (19:7-8; 7:9; Dan. 12:1-2; Matt. 25:31). I ask, what can these do? Take heart, these are not called to come and fight. MacArthur writes: "These are not coming to fight with Jesus, but to reign with Him" (MacArthur, 219).

Jesus will speak the Word of Judgment which is His sword, and the armies of the world will be destroyed on the spot. The people on the earth who are in rebellion will be destroyed in an instant. All who reject His rule will be swiftly judged. The winepress of His wrath has come to be.

As Jesus and His army come down, the angel announces to the vultures of the world, "It's supper time." Do you see the battlefield? There "Satan's fake Christ (Antichrist) has gathered the armies of the world. Psalm 2:1-3, "the nations rage, the people plot, and the kings and rulers have set themselves against Yahweh and his Messiah. We see the armies destroyed and two of the three members of the false trinity are captured and thrown into the fire." (Hamilton, 363)

Now the powers of this world will be no more. Jesus has come as a new leader to rule and reign forever more.

3. Jesus' rule is unmatched by any kingdom in history (20:1-6).

As the smoke clears from the battle, John gives us news (20:1-3) that we long to hear. **"Satan is bound for a thousand years and no longer has the ability to deceive the nations of the world."**

Brothers and sisters, this is the answer needed for our urgent prayers. No change in earthly government or new gun laws will stop the hatred and violence in our world. There must be the coming of a new leader. A leader from heaven. His name is Jesus.

Jesus is coming back to this earth, and for 1000 years, He will rule the earth. Take a moment and linger here. Imagine a world without Satan's influence. In our world, Satan deceives. The word "deceive" speaks of misleading people as to proper views they should have. Here are some examples of Satan's work, "to twist people's thoughts," "to cause what is false to seem like what is true," "to make a lie appear true," "to dig away the truth," or "to cover the eyes with lies."

Is it any wonder our world is in the shape it is in? Without the lifechanging power of Christ, the world has no hope to overcome Satan's deception, which leads to man's destruction. The Apostle John wrote:

> "¹⁸ We know that everyone who has been born of God does not keep on sinning, but he who was born of God protects him, and the evil one does not touch him. ¹⁹ We know that we are from God, and the whole world lies in the power of the evil one." (I John 5:18-19).

In the Millennial Kingdom the world will no longer be under the power of the evil one. For a 1000 years people will serve the Lord. All those who had surrendered their lives to Christ before the great battle in the Tribulation will be the citizens of the world. Also, those who had died will come to life (first resurrection) and reign with the Lord. However, those who lived and died in rebellion against the Lord will remain in the graves under the wrath of God reserved for a day and time (Great White Throne Judgment). These next words are eternally important for you to read and heed: **"Blessed and holy is the one who shares in the first resurrection! Over such the second death has no power..."**

What is the Second Death? This is so important. To answer the question, we must first define the First Death. The First Death is the death every human experiences when they die a physical death. This means the Second Death is an eternal spiritual death, which those who reject Christ will suffer for forever under the wrath of God. Here is the deal. Those who follow Christ die once and live forever in heaven. Those who reject Christ live once and die twice. The last death has no ending. It is eternity in Hell. So right now, is the only time we have.

Please do not take a chance on eternity. Follow Christ.

For 1000 years, the Lord reigns. There has been no rule like His in all of history. Now notice what happens next in (Vs: 7-10).

WE SEE AN OLD NEMESIS

At the end of this time, God releases Satan for a brief period. Notice, even a 1000-year confinement does not change Satan's viewpoint toward God. He holds the same hatred and rebellious heart he has had since he rebelled in heaven before creation. Satan is able to quickly raise an army to stand against God from all corners of the world.

Why does God allow this? This proves the condition of man's heart can only be changed by God's heart. Who are these people who are in rebellion? There is some disagreement here, but to the best of my ability I believe these people come from the ranks of those who were born during these 1000 years. Warren Wierbse comments:

> "People who have been living in a perfect environment, under the perfect government of God's Son, will finally admit the truth and rebel against the King! Their obedience will be seen as mere feigned submission, and not true faith in Christ at all." (Warren Wierbse, *The Bible Exposition Commentary* [Colorado Springs, Colorado, Victor books, 2000], 142).

An uncountable number will march with Satan. It is here where I pause and say, only those who have come to know Christ, and will come to know Christ, will follow the true leader in a different world.

The Battle does not end until we raise the white flag of surrender to Jesus Christ. Notice as this New Leader is challenged by an Old Nemesis.

WE SEE THE FINAL WORD

As the army stands behind Satan, suddenly fire comes from the heavens and consumes them. The entire army is totally exterminated by God's hand of judgment. MacArthur writes: "Their souls will go into the realm of punishment, awaiting their final sentencing to eternal Hell which is about to take place" (MacArthur, 242).

Now we read God's final word to Satan. He is cast into the lake of fire to be tormented day and night forever and ever. This is God's final word to Satan, and in short order (20:11-14) it will be God's final word to a rebellious people from all generations.

As I close this chapter, I wonder, whose army are you in? Your answer determines where you spend eternity. If you want to be in God's army, let me challenge you to turn now to the conclusion of our study and read it carefully.

STUDY QUESTIONS:

1. What characteristics of Jesus mean the most to you, and how hard is it to convince the world of who Jesus is?

2. What makes for a good leader of a nation? Is it important for a leader to be a Christ-follower? Explain your answer.

3. Why does the Bible reference Jesus' words as being a sword? Explain your answer.

4. What does the Bible mean by Jesus "ruling with a rod of iron?"

5. Explain how life will be in the 1000-year reign of Jesus.

6. Explain both the First and Second Deaths mentioned by John in chapter 20.

7. Why will so many people turn away from Jesus at the end of the 1000-year reign of Christ?

8. How powerful are the words of Jesus?

CHAPTER TWENTY-FOUR

God's Courtroom, The Final Judgement

REVELATION 20:11-15

"What we propose is to punish acts which have been regarded as criminal since the time of Cain and have been so written in every civilized code." –Supreme Court Justice, Robert Jackson

It was obvious that the war with Germany was coming to a close. The American President Franklin Roosevelt wanted to develop a plan by which the world powers would judge those who were deemed war criminals. One of the people he sought wisdom from was Supreme Court Justice Robert Jackson. The above quote was finally accepted as part of the guidelines for the famous Nuremburg Trials (1945-1949). All those who were placed on trial were, in the eyes of the world, guilty as charged, but some of those charged maintained their innocence with the foolish declaration - they were only doing their duty. But in the end, they received just judgment. I wonder if those on trial realized there was still one more judgment they would face after death.

Question: Do you realize there is one more judgment coming to every person on the earth who has rejected Jesus Christ? Do you know that the purpose of this judgment is not to determine a person's guilt or innocence, but to determine a person's level of punishment in Hell? Tony Evans pens difficult but true words: "When a person rejects God and chooses to follow Satan instead, God will not interfere. If you love the devil that much, then God will let you live with him forever." (Tony Evans, *Afterlife* [Dallas Texas, Urban alternative, 2013], 93). But be assured, the life a person will have is not of happiness, but hell itself. It is with urgency that I write this chapter believing that this truth will get on the radar of what is ahead for all those who live on the face of the earth.

In our studies, we have come to the time of this final judgment known as The Great White Throne Judgment. The 1000-year reign of Christ, with those who are from the first resurrection, has ended. Satan has been released, and those who rebelled against God have been put down. Now it is time for all men and women of every generation who have rejected Christ to come to God's judgment bar.

"This is the final bar of justice in God's plan for the inhabitants of planet earth. Unlike earthly courtrooms, there will be a Judge but no jury, a prosecutor but no defender, and a sentence but no appeal." David Jeremiah, *Escaping the Coming Night, Vol. 62*).

John begins his description of this scene with the simple words, "then I saw…" Please do not casually look at this description. It is my prayer for all who read this to either have already surrendered your life to Jesus, or to now surrender your life to King Jesus (see Conclusion to know how). For me, I know, I will only be at this judgment as an observer because I will have already been before the Judgment Seat of Christ (II Cor. 5:9-10) as one of His followers. John's observations are eternally urgent for the world to see. John writes about four things he sees in God's courtroom:

JOHN SEES THE THRONE OF JUDGMENT.

John writes of this throne as being great, which speaks about the exceeding greatness of its power. According to Rev. 4:5 this throne cannot be overthrown. John describes this throne as being white, which speaks of the purity and of the righteous judgments being delivered from this throne. From this throne comes true and impartial judgment. Just as its leader is pure, so is the throne itself (Rev. 1:14).

JOHN SEES THE PERSON RULING ON THE THRONE.

John writes, "I saw him..." Who is this person? From Jesus' own words in John 5:22 we know this is Jesus Himself who has been placed on this throne by God the Father. In Acts 10:42 Peter declares, "Christ was ordained by God to be the judge of the living and the dead."

John saw Jesus seated there. This is the Jesus we first read about in Rev. 1:5-7. He is the one who revealed God to us. He is the one who was raised from the dead. He is the one who was coming to be the Ruler of the kings of the earth. He is the one who loved the church and freed her from her sins. He is the one we are looking for to return. Consider: He is the one we look forward to returning, but He is also the One the world will dread when He comes.

Jonathan Edwards wrote: "When God holds the trial for your case...He will have no compassion upon you, He will not forbear the executions of His wrath, or in the least lighten His hand; there shall be no moderation or mercy." He will reject those who have rejected Him in their lifetime (John 5:27-30).

John comments about the earth and sky being removed. This means there will no longer be any place for the people to hide from God's presence (Rev. 6:19; 12:8).

JOHN SEES A SEA OF PEOPLE
BEFORE THE THRONE.

On Judgment Day there will be people from every walk of life. There will be those whose names we will recognize from history (great) and there will be those of whom we have no knowledge (small). They will be resurrected from their burial places (20:5). The seas will give up their dead. All those killed in wars, floods, drownings, on battlefields and in the forgotten places of the world will be resurrected. All will be resurrected to stand in judgment for the deeds of their lives.

Maybe you ask, where have the souls of these people been? They have been in Hades (the realm of the dead (Luke 16:19-25). They have been awaiting the final sentencing of God.

I see them standing there. Adolf Hitler is in that line and so is a grandmother who baked cookies for the neighborhood kids but never surrendered her life to Jesus Christ.

As they stand there before Jesus, books are opened. There has been much discussion and debate about the books and what they are. Here is what we know for sure: God's standard for life, called the Bible, will be there. We know the Lamb's Book of life that has recorded all the redeemed of the ages is there.

David Jeremiah lists five other books that he believes are there: "According to Romans 2:15 there could be the book of conscience which reveals the times our conscience failed to do what is right. According to Matthew 12:36-37, the book of words could be there. This book has all we have ever said in it. According to Romans 2:16, there could be the book of secret works which contains all the things we have done that we do not want others to know about. According to II Corinthians 11:15, there is the book of our public works. Then finally there is the book of life, Dan. 12:1, which has the record of our existence on the earth." (David Jeremiah, 64-66).

As I consider the books, I realize there will be no way to lie out of, make excuses for, or deny the events and actions of life. It is all there to clearly see. Question: What is in the books about your life and my life? Do you want to stand before this judgment? I do not want to stand there, and by His grace and mercy I will not stand there.

JOHN SEES THE LAKE OF FIRE.

Do you see the Lake of Fire? This is John's description of Hell. "Hell is the wasteland outside of God's goodness where there is no exit and no change." (Tony Evans, Pg. 100) Consider this question, who goes to this place? John writes: "anyone whose name is not found in the Lamb's Book of Life." The word "found" is the same word used in Luke 15 to describe the searching for the lost sheep, lost coin, and the lost son. Even at the Great White Throne we see the love and mercy of God, in that God genuinely searches for the names of those who stand before Him. In this moment the following words are more than appropriate, "such are without excuse."

Oh, my heart breaks as I see wave after wave of people being cast alive into the torment of the lake of fire. This place is where there will be weeping and gnashing of teeth (Matt. 13:42). There will be fire that is unquenchable (Matt. 25:41). In comparison, if you have ever been burned, you know the pain, but you also know how it felt when the pain was taken care of. It will never be this way in Hell.

Maybe you ask, "Do you really believe in Hell?" Yes, I believe in Hell because Jesus said there was a Hell (Matt. 18:8-9). Jesus spoke far more about Hell than He did Heaven. If there was no Hell to be delivered from, there would have been no need for Jesus to come and give His life on the cross (John 3:16). Maybe you ask, "How could a loving God create such a place?" You need to know God did not create Hell for people. He created it for Satan and his demons (Matt. 25:41,46).

Not only are people cast into Hell, but death itself and Hades (the holding tank for the dead) is now cast into the Lake of Fire. The experience of death and judgment will be no more for the people of God. However, perpetual death and Hell will be the eternal existence of those who have rejected Jesus. It is shocking truth, but the lost world will be in torment with Satan, the Beast, and the False Prophet.

News records from the days of the Nuremberg Trials tell the story of some who were tried, being defiant until the moment of their execution. I wonder, what is your mindset as we approach the day when the Lord will return to judge the living and the dead? I pray you take seriously what we have read, and I pray you receive Jesus' payment for your sin so that you will not appear at this judgment.

STUDY QUESTIONS:

1. Do you believe in a literal Heaven and Hell? Defend your answer.

2. Why do only 7% of Americans believe in a literal Hell?

3. Are there any parts of this judgment that trouble you?

4. Do you believe there are different degrees of punishment in Hell? Defend your answer.

5. Why do people often think there will not be a judgment for their deeds?

6. Describe Heaven and Hell to the best of your ability.

7. What type of questions will the Lord ask on Judgment Day? Give examples.

8. Where will you be and where will your family members be on Judgment Day?

CHAPTER TWENTY-FIVE

Living Between Two Worlds

REV. 21:1-9

"Never shall I forget that night, the first night in camp, that turned my life into one long night seven times sealed...." –Elie Wiesel

"Never shall I forget that smoke. Never shall I forget the small faces of the children whose bodies I saw transformed into smoke under a silent sky. Never shall I forget those flames that consumed my faith forever. Never shall I forget the nocturnal silence that deprived me for all eternity of the desire to live. Never shall I forget those moments that murdered my God and my soul and turned my dreams to ashes." (Elie Wiesel, *Night* [New York, Hill and Wang, 2006], 19).

His writing still haunts my soul after all these years. I still remember in 2008 reading Elie Wiesel (Holocaust survivor's) first-hand account of the evil of the Holocaust. Elie's own personal journey strikes at the core of how evil can become our world. His is not the only story of evil and unjust activity in our world. We live in a day when it seems that evil is all around us.

Question: "What type of world do we live in?" The Apostle Paul writes about a world that is getting worse and worse. The direction of our world leads many people to true discouragement and even disillusionment with the world. Elie Wiesel over and over asked one question, "Where is God in this world?"

For me, this is a fair question, and for God, this is a question He answers for us in the Book of Revelation. The Lord Jesus is preparing for us a place in heaven, and He is coming again to judge the world and to establish His rule and reign forever. With urgency in my heart, I want to anticipate the question that now comes. I know, you may be asking, "But what about right now, Keith. How do I live now as I wait?"

I believe you and I must live as Christ-followers who genuinely embrace a life of living between two worlds. David Platt explained it this way: "Christians are pilgrims are on a journey to Heaven. We live between the time of Christ's First Coming and His Second-Coming." (Platt, David. Sermon "Consummation of the Kingdom" October 28,. Knowing this - leads us to both endure this life and to live with expectancy of the life that is to come.

As we come to Revelation 21, we read of John's seeing that world to come. As John describes the world to come, we see both good news and bad news for the people who live on the earth. First, there is the good news:

HEAVEN IS COMING FOR
THE CHILD OF GOD

Please take a moment and re-read the good news. Heaven is coming for the Child of God! After the world is judged at the Great White throne, the Bible says the first earth and the first heaven went away.

The earth we know (originally created by God as recorded in Genesis 1-2) which has endured 6000 plus years of abuse by humanity and then will endure the wrath of God (Rev. 6-19) being poured out against humanity, will now be totally released from the curse placed upon it (Gen. 3:15-18). Revelation 22:3 says, "No longer will there be any curse."

On this earth, evil exists and Satan reigns. Each day - the heaven grows dark at night and all kinds of evil takes place (John 3:18-19). But in that day, the good news is, there will be no more evil and no more darkness. Life as we know it will be no more. John writes about the sea going away. "Ours is presently a water-based environment. All the earth is dependent on water for survival. But believers' bodies will not require water like they do now" (MacArthur, 263).

The earth and the heavens will be new. But we also see the New Jerusalem coming down out of heaven. This will be the capital city of the new earth. This news was so great that a loud voice from heaven cried out, "Behold...."

Here we long for a closer walk with the Lord, and we long to always be in His presence. The good news is, when Heaven comes, so comes the Lord Jesus to dwell with us. Yes, God will be with us in fellowship, in praise, in direction, in love, and in all wisdom. Think about it. There will be no more, "I don't know why this happened," or "Why didn't this happen?"

The joy of this news gets even deeper as John writes about what our Lord will do when He arrives: He will wipe away all those things that cause tears in our eyes. Death causes tears, but there are no grave markers there or need for funeral services (I Cor. 15:26). Death is no more, so no more crying over death. There will be no more sin so there will be no more blowing it with God. In this, God wipes away the tears from mourning. Tragedy and disease also cause tears, but in that place called Heaven all tragedy and disease disappear (Is. 35:10). In this world we have pain from sickness, injury, and emotional and physical abuse. But not there, all sources of pain are wiped away (Is. 51:11) so there is no more pain. I cannot help but write, "Praise God," because all the former things are going away. The old life and the old nature are gone forever (Is. 65:19-25).

Brothers and sisters, there could not be better news than to hear that someday we will lay down all the burdens of this world. The truth is, we can lay them down at Jesus' feet even now (Matt. 11:28-30). Our Lord is a burden bearer, and He is a burden lifter (I Peter 5:6-7). We can live with joy now, knowing pain will end, and problems are being worked out by our Lord.

You ask, "Are you sure? Is it real? Can I trust what you are writing?" Oh, my friend, it's not what I say, I am simply writing down what Jesus said. And Jesus said, you can trust that He will make it happen. The same God who redeemed you from sin is coming to rescue you from this sin-sick world. The God who is making people new (II Cor. 5:17) is coming to make a new world. Jesus said, "It's done! I said it, and it will come to be."

In this moment, Heaven issues an invitation for people who are weary of the gods and godlessness of this world. Jesus says from the throne, "Come to me." The phrase, "you who thirst," refers to those who recognize their desperate spiritual need" (MacArthur, 271). Just like the woman at the well (John 4) whose thirst for the world left her with multiple divorces and destitute of joy, God offers you a joy the world cannot offer. Jesus is "living water" (Jn. 7:37-38). Jesus offers you a life that begins here and finds its ultimate fulfillment in Heaven. If you thirst for the true God and for the true peace He offers, receive

His salvation (Rom. 10:13). It is free, and it is for you and whoever believes in Jesus.

This water is also for those of us who sometimes drink in the stale water of this world. We sometimes get flooded with evil and mistreatment and unfair practices at work, school, in government, and sometimes even in church. Jesus is the "fountain of living water" (Jer. 2:13) who calls us to drink deeply in the well of His salvation day after day.

Dr. Hamilton writes, "The only thing that qualifies you for a drink is thirsting for it. Thirsting for it though, means thirsting for God. It you thirst for other things; you don't thirst for this" (Hamilton, 387).

Notice Heaven's word to those who conquer (those who are faithful). Yes, this world is tough, but the eternal life we are going to experience in heaven makes this life seem much more bearable.

Now we come to the bad news:

HELL IS AWAITING THOSE
WHO REJECT JESUS

Verse eight begins with the word "but." This word moves us from the good news to the bad news. Not everyone is going to Heaven when Jesus comes. Heaven is adamant about this truth. Who are those people who are not going? John gives us a list: Those who are cowardly, which means those who will not take a stand for Jesus. Those who are faithless, meaning those who will not believe in Jesus as their Lord and Savior. Those who are detestable, meaning those who are vile in their wickedness - such people have no refrain from open sin. Those who are murderers and take the life of others through many different means. Those who follow the spirit world controlled by Satan. The list ends with those who worship other gods and those who live their lives filled with lies.

Question: Do you see yourself on this list? I must be honest, I used to be on that list until I met Jesus Christ as my Lord and Savior. From the moment of my conception, Hell was awaiting me. But thanks be to God, Jesus came to my rescue. He opened my eyes to my need of Him. In February 1974, Jesus Christ became the boss of my life. From that day to this day, Heaven has been coming for me.

A lot has happened in this world since 1974, but certainly not like what happened in the Holocaust. I think of 9-11-2001, which drastically changed our world. Many other events have affected the world we live in. But personally, for you who read this, there have been many events that have changed your world and your outlook toward the future. I wish I could make your past hurts be as if they had never been, but I cannot. I wish I could shield you from future hurts, but I cannot. However, I can do one thing. I can give you the good news of a world coming that will wipe away all your hurts, habits, and hang-ups.

But I also must give you the bad news - all the tough moments you have faced in this life are nothing compared to the Hell that awaits you if you keep on rejecting Jesus as Lord and Savior. All who reject Jesus will have their own personal place in the Lake of Fire. I am rejoicing today that there is no personal place for me in Hell, and I pray there will be no place for you as well. The choice is yours. Please say yes to Jesus.

STUDY QUESTIONS:

1. Why are there so many acts of violence in our world today?

2. How does Jesus' presence in our trials make life so much more bearable?

3. Why do tough and tragic moments have such a lasting effect on people's lives?

4. When will the Lord return, and why do you want Him to return?

5. What does it mean "to thirst for God?"

6. How does God do away with the old earth and create a new earth?

7. Why does God stress He is "trustworthy and true?"

8. Why do people who know about the bad news, still reject the good news of Jesus Christ?

CHAPTER TWENTY-SIX

I'm Going Home

REVELATION 21:9-22:5

"The country went mad with joy. People were
dancing in the streets, both wealthy and the poor. Adults acting
like children hugging each other, and throwing their hats in the air.
For in Denmark the war was finally over."

I have watched videos of the moments when nations were liberated at the end of World War II. I have read story after story of people who had been exiled and upon hearing of their opportunity to go home, broke out with a joy that is beyond understanding, unless you had been in their place. Most of those in exile said, it was only the prospect of going home that kept them going in the war.

Honest admission, I have in times past gone through entire weeks without even once thinking about Heaven. This is honest, but hard to admit, because I have just admitted that I am sometimes extremely attached to this world. Scripture teaches us of the sinfulness of this viewpoint. For example, II Tim. 2:4 "do not become entangled in civilian pursuits." Also, there is Colossians 3:2, "Set your minds on things above, not on things that are on the earth."

David Jeremiah writes: "We may want to go to Heaven someday, but we may think, let that someday be when I'm very, very old and have done everything on this earth I want to do." "Escaping the Coming Night, Pg. 291."

Question: Does the prospect of Heaven in the next twenty-four hours excite you? Now I am not making a prediction, I am leading you to understand where we are in the church world today. I truly believe our answer to the question depends on the status of our heart, mind, and present circumstances. In Philippians 3:21, Paul was "eagerly awaiting our Savior." In II Tim. 4:7, Paul was ready to go to Heaven. His warfare was at the end. The world held no sway over him. In Paul's mind, what was waiting was far better than what was in his present life.

One might wonder, is it really important that I have Heaven on my mind as a Christ-follower? John MacArthur writes: "Believers who do not have Heaven on their minds trivialize their lives, hinder the power of the church, and become absorbed with the fading things of this world." Cited from Pg. 260, IBID. Think with me about how much emphasis is placed on building our individual kingdoms here. Often people cannot give to or be a part of a local church because all they possess is invested in the trivial things of this world. Consider how often we fail to think about the wonder of Heaven as a reason to invite people to Jesus. Finally, how many times do people end up trapped and abused by the world system that promised them Heaven on earth?

In Revelation 21 we read John's glorious description of Heaven. Earlier in chapter 21 (Vs: 2-3) John declares there will be a new Heaven and a new earth. Now John describes the new Jerusalem which is the headquarters of Heaven coming down to the new earth. As I read this description, I am quickly pulled away from the fading luster of this world, and I become keenly connected to the world to come. I can say with the greatest of honesty, I am longing to go home! I woke up this morning wondering, could this be the day that I will go home?

Let me challenge you to look deeper at Heaven in this chapter, and let me compel you to surrender your life to Jesus, if you have not, so that you can become a resident there. Follow me as we focus on four observations from the text about Heaven:

The breath-taking view of Heaven (21:9-21)

Before John sees the headquarters of Heaven (New Jerusalem) he is pointed to seeing the Bride (the church). It is those who have followed Christ who are the people who will live with God serving Him and worshipping Him in this city. Brothers and sisters, I will be in that city. My parents and my grandparents will be in that city. Peter, James, John, and all the disciples will be in that city.

This is a breathtaking place. I wish I could point out to you in this devotion all the features of this city, but let us choose just a few:

- The glory of God - This represents the brightness of all His attributes. Wherever you look and wherever you go, you see His glory radiating from the city. We will see the glory Jesus spoke about in John 17:24. This is so important to me, knowing how dark of a world we live in today. This is so important to me, because there are days when I get discouraged by the disease and death here on the earth. The evil deeds of men sometimes leave us in fear, but not in that place. His glory will remind us, this is Heaven for eternity.

- The foundations of the city with the names of the Apostles written on them - This foundation reminds me of Jesus' words in Matt. 16:18, "I will build my church and the gates of Hell will not prevail." Here on the earth, ministries sometimes crumble. Such ministries have leaders who fall prey to the pull of the world. I see Christian marriages that breakup because someone got off the foundation of Jesus. But when Christians build their lives on Jesus, nothing can topple us (Matt. 7:23-27). The foundations are a reminder that Heaven is coming, and Hell cannot and will not win.

• The size of the capital city – This is beyond my understanding. Someone did the math. Just the base area of the city would be 1,750,329 square miles. Think about it. This place is so large that the saved of all ages will be able to live there. I think of Heaven in these terms, there is still room for more. Jesus' words in Luke 14:23, "Go out to the highways and hedges and compel people to come in, that my house may be filled." There is room in Heaven for you.

• The riches of Heaven are seen in its design with material of jasper, emerald, pearl, and gold to just name a few. Brothers and sisters, who could worry and feel mistreated by God on this earth? Look what we will have in Heaven that will never fade away. There are no U-Hauls lined up in Heaven to take our treasure away.

The brightness of Heaven, (21:22-27)

In our world we need the sun and moon. We could not survive without the blessings of God in giving us the greater and lesser lights (Gen. 1:17-18). Both the moon and sun work together to give us seasons, time, direction on the earth, warmth, health, and so many other things. God's wisdom in the sun and moon amazes me. For example, it takes the earth 365 days to make one revolution around the sun, and the moon moves counter-clockwise around the earth every 29 days. Without them, our world would be chaotic in many ways. We would not survive. But in the new Heaven, it is God who is the light we need. Finally, we will see how God rules in the affairs of men. We will see time differently, and we will have no night there. God's glory lights our way.

In the Bible, darkness is symbolic of sin (John 3:18-19). There will be no sin (nothing unclean) in Heaven. It will be totally bright with daytime never ending. This means for me, no fear in Heaven. We will rest and be new for eternity.

Does anyone want to go yet?

The blessing of life in Heaven, (22:1-2)

Oh my friend, how could Heaven offer us anymore than we have already seen? But wait, there is more! We see the blessing of life both in its quality and its duration. First, we see its quality. When Jesus met the Woman at the Well, He offered her living water (John 4:10-12). When Jesus stood at the conclusion of the Feast of Booths (John 7:37-39), He said, "If anyone thirsts, let him come to me and drink." In Christ, the Woman at the Well received new life and a quality of life (spiritual life) she never had before. Here in Heaven, is the eternal stream of life that reminds us of the quality of life that never will run dry.

We also see something we have not seen since the Garden of Eden. We see the Tree of Life (Gen. 2:9; 3:22-24). "This tree symbolized the blessing of eternal life,". This tree also speaks about our quality of life. Hamilton writes, "The redeemed enjoy the new and better Eden, old hurts will be healed. The nationalism, the racism, the acrimony, the bitterness, and the long history of warfare will be healed. This also reminds us, there is only one way back to Eden, trusting Christ as Lord and Savior." (Hamilton Pg. 404)

The beauty of God Himself, (22:3-5)

Brothers and sisters, the Bible says, "We will see His face." Yes, I will, in person, see Jesus. The Apostle John promised us this in I John 3:2, "Beloved, we are God's children now, and what we will be has not yet appeared; but we know that when he appears we shall be like him, because we shall see him as he is. I can't wait to see Jesus and fall before Him, and, as I would do for no other man, I will worship Him. I will sing praise to His name. I will revere Him as my King who is coming to reign forever and ever.

There is so much I have said to Jesus in prayer, but to be literally in His physical presence makes glory bumps come up on my arms. I will worship at the feet of the one who has removed the curse (2:17). I will worship before the God who has been my light (Ps. 119:105) for all these years. I will worship before the God who has met every need. Every Child of God will be with Him forever.

So I ask again, anyone want to go to Heaven? If so, Jesus is your guide, and He is the only way to get there. Someone said, "If we are too heavenly minded we are of no earthly good." After reading these verses, I would have to disagree, because what I have learned leads me to be a far more passionate worshipper, worker, and witness for Christ on this old and broken earth. Is it of any wonder why so many come to the place where they say, I want to go home?

STUDY QUESTIONS:

1. How have your views concerning Heaven been altered by this study?

2. Why do some people not believe in Heaven?

3. How does it make you feel to realize Heaven will not be everyone's home?

4. Describe what drinking from the water of life means?

5. Why will there be no need for the sun and moon in Heaven?

6. What will it be like to see Jesus for the first time?

7. How does the reality of Heaven change the way you live here?

8. How would you describe Heaven to a non-believer?

CHAPTER TWENTY-SEVEN

What Are My Options?

REVELATION 22:6-21

*"And behold, I am coming soon. Blessed is the one who keeps the words
of the prophecy of this book." –Revelation 22:7*

As you begin to read this chapter, I hope you have the same amount of excitement as I have in writing this chapter. I think about all we have read, and I think about all that is soon to happen in our world. I can hardly contain the excitement I have, because I know what awaits the church of the Lord Jesus Christ. At the same time, I have sorrow in my heart because I know there are so many people in the world who have chosen to reject the God who says, "I am coming soon."

As I consider what I have learned, I look at my life, and I wonder how much time do I have left before the Lord returns? With those thoughts, I anxiously look to the last chapter of this book to discover what my options are in these last days.

The Apostle John knew what his options were. He could either write what God told him to write or he could not write what God told him to write. I am so glad he chose the correct option; John accepted his role of writing down (for all to know) what God had said to Him (Rev. 1:1-2,19). John was faithful in making seven copies of the vision, and he sent them to seven churches. These churches were called to follow the commands of the Lord (Rev. 2-3). It was these seven churches who were the first to hear about the Great Tribulation, The unholy trinity, the Battle of Armageddon, and the Second Coming. It was these churches who heard more about Heaven than any generation before them.

These seven churches had options before them, they could either keep the news to themselves or they could spread the news. I am so glad they did not keep the news to themselves.

As John completes his writing, he continues to record what he has heard. "The angel said, 'these words are trustworthy and true...'" The same God who inspired (NLT) the prophets, sent his angels to tell the church (servants) what is to come. John records, "These things are soon to be." Brothers and sisters, because we know these things are coming, surely it must fuel our decision-making process. In these last verses there are no less than three options before the world.

"One can either take these things seriously or not seriously." 22:7-9

The one who is trustworthy and true says, "I am coming shortly." This coming is to be taken seriously. Jesus says, you who are on the earth, hear Me, I am coming to where you are. Brothers and sisters, when you see the signs, He is coming shortly.

For me, I want to take all of this seriously, because I am a planner. I try to plan for everything. Now I know there are things we cannot plan for. Death will come when God plans it, (Job 14:4-5). The Lord's return date will also happen on God the Father's timetable (Matt. 24:31-32).

Sadly, people take other things far more seriously than they do the Word of the Lord. For example, as I write this, it is six days until the beginning of College Football season. Already the sports world is chanting, "Countdown to Kickoff." Brothers and sisters, John is saying it's countdown to Jesus' return.

For a lost world who does not take this seriously, there will be a day when they will see their option as a mistake. It is only those who chose Christ who will be "happy" (blessed) when the Lord returns. John was so serious that we see him falling before the angel to give praise. But the angel says, "worship God." God's call on our lives is to worship Him. We are to give our allegiance to Him alone.

"One can make changes or not make changes." 22:10-16

Next the angel says, openly make this known to everyone. The time is near (KJV "At hand"). I would say, the clock is ticking.

For those who are planners, when the clock begins you are out of the gate working on the project and making changes all along the way. For those who are last minute people, you also know the clock is ticking, but you are not used to making a plan or changes early on the clock. You know what you want to do, but you have other things that are already counting down. What are your options? You can wait to the last minute and follow Jesus. Say you are going to follow, but wait to the end to make the changes, or you can decide to not change at all.

As I read Revelation 22:11, it seems that John only gives two options for planners and last minute people. Here are the two options, either continue to live in the world, with its evil and unrighteous ways, or make the changes needed in order to follow Jesus.

John's words in this verse seem hard and unmerciful, but they are not. The context actually reveals the opposite. John is attempting to warn humanity, before the Great Tribulation comes, of their need to follow Jesus. If the cross does not change a person's heart, he or she will certainly not be changed by anything else. Neither the threat of tribulation, return of the Lord, or the Great White Throne Judgment will change them.

"Jesus has already stepped out of Heaven and come to this earth's abuse. Jesus was nailed to a hellish instrument called the cross, and He died in agony. With every drop of His blood, He was saying, I love you, and I want to save you. My friend, if you die and go to Hell, you will have to climb over the battered, bruised body of Jesus to get there. All along the way Jesus is shouting, Stop, don't go to Hell." (Rogers, Pg. 296)

John knows those who reject Jesus will not change in the Tribulation period. This is God's warning to make the changes now. When the Lord returns, He will come to reward all people for what they have done in their lifetime. In particular, Jesus is coming to reward two groups.

He will reward those who made the changes (such people washed their robes by submitting to Jesus who washes them clean from their sins, Eph. 1:7; Rev. 7:14). Once such people are made clean, they continue to clean out the outside of their lives. Christians continue to change day by day as they are striving to follow the commandments of God. Such people have a place reserved for them in Heaven.

Jesus will not reward those who do not make changes (such people are still outside the Family of God). Such people still live an unrighteous life. Such people are making zero changes, because they continue to follow the course of this world (Eph. 2:1-3). Such people have opportunity after opportunity, but they still say "no" over and over again.

As I write these words, the Devil tries to remind me of my life when I was still outside the Family of God and times when I have failed in the Family of God. But in the same moment, the Lord speaks loudly and says, "What sin? My Son paid the debt for your sin (I John 1:7). Look at your life now and the many changes you have made which are proof that you are following me."

"One can live life for God or not for God." 22:17-21

Brothers and sisters, there is one more option before us. Notice what the Holy Spirit and the Church of the Lord Jesus (Bride) are calling out, "Come." These two are calling to the root and descendant of David and the Bright and Morning Star to come. To call someone a star is to exalt them (Dan. 12:3). Jesus is the exalted one who existed before David and came to be our Savior and shortly He is returning to be our King. The Holy Spirit and the church are calling for Jesus to come.

Hear these words, we only invite someone over if we want them to come and if we are ready for them to come. If one chooses the option of living for God, he or she will be ready at any moment to welcome King Jesus.

However, if you have been drinking all the polluted water of this world, you might not have a thirst for Jesus. You certainly will not even understand what the Water of Life even tastes like. However, there is still time to choose a different option. Here is the last invitation of the Bible. Humanity is offered the option for one last time, come to Jesus. Jesus is the Water of Life. He offers salvation free to all who will follow Him.

John's words are followed up with a warning, do not mess up the Word of God. To those who do, the consequences are devastating. John understood the Word of God alone has the ability to convert the soul. This book, God's Word, is not a novel. It is not the "Left Behind" series nor is it this book you are reading that converts the soul. It is God's Word that has the power we need to direct us to the correct eternal options. Even as I write this book, I write with fear and reverence in commenting about God's Word.

Now pay close attention with me to the last words of Jesus found in the Bible. Let this soak in. The last divinely inspired words from heaven are these, "Surely I am coming soon."

These words are what defines and fuels the urgency of my life. Surely the Lord is coming soon. Yes, everything you have read is coming true. Jesus is coming soon. When you see the signs, know Jesus is coming soon. When you read Scripture, know Jesus is coming soon. In the midst of the chaos of a wicked world, be reminded Jesus is coming soon. In the cold nights of your trials be reminded Jesus is coming soon. When you are in the summertime of life, don't forget, Jesus is coming soon. When you start to lose health and when you come to the end, take heart Jesus is coming soon.

Yes, it is true, but is it true in your life? The options are before you. What will you choose?

STUDY QUESTIONS:

1. What is the hardest prophecy in Revelation to believe?

2. Defend why you either believe or do not believe all of Scripture is true.

3. Why is it so important to believe Jesus could return in our lifetime?

4. Why do so many people reject the gospel so easily?

5. What changes do you need to make in your life in light of the Second Coming of Jesus?

6. What are the signs that might be pointing to Jesus' return?

7. Why do some Christians fear the Lord's Second Coming?

8. Why does the church so seldom teach or emphasize the Lord's return?

9. Who will you share what you have learned in this study with?

Conclusion

"The path of Christianity does not lift Christians above life;
it sweeps them into life's currents, fully alive to both their exterior
world and their interior response." – Paul Miller

I f the Lord does not return by the time you receive this study, this will be my fifth time, in twenty-seven years of ministry, to complete a study of the book of Revelation. I still have all the notes from each time God has led me to prepare and then preach through the book of Revelation. When I look back at the notes from my first time working through the book, I realize, I was completely just writing down what others said. To be transparent, some of it was really good and some, let's say, I did not use the next time around.

I also noticed in my notes, that each time I studied, there was a deeper urgency in my writing. I confess, the last time, six years ago, I did not think I could be more urgent. But I can truly say, my urgency now is more than it has ever been.

As I sit at my desk, I look to my left at a map of the world that hangs on my wall. I now read the book of Revelation with the people of the world in mind. I look at the far northern tip of the map and cry out for the people of Russia. I look at New Zealand, and I pray for their souls. I look into Asia where there are the most amount of people, and I cry out; how can we reach them now? I gaze into the middle east, and I wonder, do they even know the end is coming? I look at Africa and I wonder; how many have never even heard the gospel once. Next, I turn my attention back to America and the 378 million people who make up four percent of the world's population. I pray with urgency, Lord we want to make a difference now!

As you come to the end of this study, I want to ask you a personal question: In what ways has this study generated an urgency in you? Paul Miller is so spot on when he comments about true Christianity "leading a person to being swept into life's currents."

If you are a Child of God, you should be swept into a view that says, I want to reach people now. I know this to be true in the life of my son, John, who upon graduating high school said, "Dad, why do I have to go to college, I want to make a difference now." The truth is, Revelation leads Christians into the center stage of life where we press into the work of reaching people with the gospel of Jesus Christ.

If you are not a Christ-follower, I want to share with you how you can become a Christ-follower today. First you need to know God created this world, and He is lord over the creation, Genesis 1-2. When God created this world, He created it good. But the first man and woman walked away from God, Romans 5:12. These two believed their own way was better than God's plan, Prov. 14:12. God judged Adam and Eve by placing them under His curse and wrath. Why did God do this? The truth is, they became rebels, Romans 6:23. From that moment forward, every person born has entered life as a rebel who does not seek God, Rom. 3:10-18. But God loved humanity so much that He sent Jesus to take humanity's curse and wrath, II Cor. 5:20-21; John 3:16. Now it possible to be forgiven of our rebellion, I John 1:7. I have good news for you: all who place their faith and trust in Jesus will be forgiven and become possessors of eternal life, Eph. 1:7. If you will surrender your life to Jesus, forgiveness, eternal life, and a different life will be yours now. Today I want to challenge you to pray the following prayer in true faith in Jesus:

- Jesus, I know you are God, and I know that you became a man to take my place on the cross. II Cor. 5:21

- Jesus, I know you lived, died, were buried, and rose again on the third day. I Cor. 15:1-4

- Jesus, forgive me of my sins. I repent of the wickedness of my rebellion. Luke 13:3

- Jesus, come into my life and be Lord and Savior. John 3:16

- Jesus, I want to live for you. Mark 8:34-35

- Jesus, I will tell my friends about you. I Peter 3:15

Now that you have prayed this prayer, we as fellow Christians want to help you. You can email us at *info@jacksonfbc.com* so that we can come along side of you in this new life.

For those of you who are Christ-followers, I want to challenge you with three takeaways from our studies in the book of Revelation:

1. Close out all outstanding accounts with God.

If there is any sin in your life that you are holding onto or any un-forgiveness in your heart, deal with it now. You have no time to lose. Soon you will be standing before His Judgment Seat   (II Cor. 5:9-10). There is no sin or grudge that is worth losing rewards in Heaven.

2.   Complete all outstanding assignments.

If the Lord has called you to a task for Him, now is the time to complete it. You do not want to stand before God with blood on your hands. You do not want to experience Heaven without your fellow man. You also do not want to stand before God and realize you wasted your life in matters that really did not count. Now is the time to be-come active in local, national, and global missions. All points on the compass need the gospel.

3.   Concentrate on the fact Jesus is coming again.

When I realize Jesus is coming, I move from a person who is kind of reaching out, to being a person who is completely engaged in this world, fighting for the souls of men. It is true, this day is all I know for sure I have. I really don't know if I am going to finish out this day, so I only have this moment. How can I say with the church, "Come Lord Jesus," unless I am doing my part in making ready a people to meet Him?

Thank you for joining me on this urgent journey. May you not file this book away on your shelf. May you read it again and again to stir your urgency for this day. I pray you also purchase copies to give to others who either need the Lord or are in need of a return to urgency of faith.

I say with the Holy Spirit and with the Church, "Come Lord Jesus!"

Pastor Keith

Revelation 22:20 "Surely I (Jesus) am coming soon."

August 2019

Works Cited

Akin, Daniel. *Five Who Changed The World.* Southeastern Baptist Theological Seminary, Wake Forest, NC, 2008.

Bright, Bill & Damoose John. *Red Sky in the Morning,* Orlando Florida, New Life Publications, 1998.

Carter, Matt, & Ivey Aaron. *Steal Away Home,* Nashville Tennessee, B & H Publishing group, 2017.

Dever, Mark. *What is a Healthy Church?* Wheaton Illinois, Crossway Books, 2007.

Evans, Tony. *The Afterlife, glimpses of heaven and hell.* Dallas Tx. The Urban Alternative, 2013.

Ham, Ken. *Gospel Rest.* Green Forest, Ar. Master Books, 2018.

Hamilton, James M. *Revelation, Preaching the Word,* Wheaton, Ill. Crossway Publishing, 2012.

Jeremiah, David. *Escaping the Coming Night, Vol. 4 study guide.* San Diego, Ca. Turning Point for God. 2011.

Lawson, Steve. *Philippians for You*. North America: The Good Book Company. 2017

Lord, Walter. *The Miracle of Dunkirk*, New York, New York. Open Road Media.

MacArthur, John. *MacArthur New Testament Commentary, Revelation*. Chicago: Moody Publishers, 1999.

Miller Paul E. *J Curve, Dying and Rising with Jesus in Everyday Life*. Wheaton, Illinois: Crossway, 2019

Norman, Elizabeth. *We Band of Angels*, United States, Random House Publishers, 2013.

Olson, Lynne. *Last Hope Island*, New York, Random House Publishers, 2017.

O'Reilly, Bill and & Dugard, Martin. *Killing Patton*, New York, New York. Henry Holt and Company, LLC, 2014.

Rainer, Thom. *Autopsy of a Deceased Church*, Nashville, Tennessee: B and H Publishing, 2014.

Rogers, Adrian. *Unveiling the End Times in our Time*, Nashville, Tennessee, B and H Publishing, 2004.

Sandys, Jonathan & Henley, Wallace. *God and Churchill*. Tyndale Momentum Publishing, 2015.

Shelly, Bruce. *Church History in Plain Language*, Nashville, Thomas Nelson Publishing, 2013.

Swindoll, Charles. *Insights from Revelation*. Grand Rapids Michigan, 2011.

Walvoord, John. *Revelation, In the Bible Knowledge Commentary: an exposition of the Scriptures.* Wheaton Il. Victor Books, 1985.

Wiesel, Elie. *Night.* New York, Hill and Wang publishing, 2006

Wiersbe, Warren. *The Bible Knowledge Commentary, Vol. 2,* Colorado Springs, Colorado, Victor Books, 2000.

www.ingramcontent.com/pod-product-compliance
Lightning Source LLC
LaVergne TN
LVHW051230080426
835513LV00016B/1500